I0558690

Clean Cuts

Volume 1

Clean Cuts

Volume 1

Faith-Inspired and Family-Friendly
Monologues for Film, TV, and Stage

Grace Covington

Library of Congress Control Number: Pending

ISBN 979-8-9925861-1-4 (Paperback)
ISBN 979-8-9925861-2-1 (Hardcover)
ISBN 979-8-9925861-0-7 (eBook)

Published by Grace Lerone Publishing

PRINTED IN THE UNITED STATES OF AMERICA

Cover design by Eric L. Covington

For permissions, inquiries, or bookings, contact: GraceLeronePublishing@gmail.com

First Edition

Acknowledgments

First and foremost, I give all glory and thanks to God, My LORD and Co-Author. He is the source of every good thing in my life. He provided the vision, the words, and the ability to bring it all together. I am grateful for His guidance, wisdom, and endless provision. Thank you, Jesus!

To my amazing husband Eric, thank you for your love, support, and belief in me. Your creativity shines, and I'm especially grateful for the beautiful book cover you designed for me. I am honored to be your wife.

To my parents, Mom, thank you for pushing me to finish this book and reminding me that I could do it. Dad, I loved seeing your excitement with every monologue I shared. Your enthusiasm made the process even more rewarding.

To my brother and sister-in-love, you are both such a blessing in my life. To my niece and nephew, always remember that you can do anything you set your mind to. Your joy and love inspire me every day. Thank you for letting me include your dogs in this book: Sasha, who will always be remembered, and Dash, the new lively addition to the family.

To my Goddaughter Alissa, whose birthday happens to be the same day as this book's release; I hope this serves as a reminder that with God, all things are possible. May you always chase your dreams with faith and confidence.

To my Powerhouse Sisterhood Suite sisters, thank you for your faith, talent, and encouragement. Your support and inspiration have been invaluable, and I'm so grateful to have you all in my life.

A special thank you to Beverly Holloway Shuey. Your monologue showcases planted the seed for this book, and I deeply appreciate the work you do to uplift and create opportunities for actors.

And to every reader: whether you are an actor preparing for a performance or someone who simply enjoys a great story, thank you. Your support means the world to me, and I pray that this book inspires, equips, and encourages you on your journey.

With Gratitude,
Grace Covington

Contents

Introduction   1

Faith-Based Dramatic Monologues   2

A Miracle on the Doorstep   3
The Right Thing   4
Melting Faith   5
Riding the Storm   6
I'm Here, Dad   7
Rising from the Rubble   8
Grandma's Recipe   9
I'm Tired of This   10
Forgiving the Unforgivable   11
This Is Our Moment   12
Is She the One?   13
Always a Bridesmaid   14
Breaking the Cycle   15
The First Day   16
Honoring God's Call   17
A Brother's Goodbye   18
Behind the Mask   19
The Right Bait   20
Strength in Weakness   21
The Crumb Snatcher   22
Until We Meet Again   23
Reflection of Faith   24
The Finish Line   25
A Heart Set Apart   26
Don't Jump   27

Faith-Based Comedic Monologues

Faith-Based Comedic Monologues   28

Mistaken Generosity   29
Mime for a Change   30
I'm a Glutton   31
Fishing in the Storm   32
Is He the One?   33
Making Waves   34
Grace at the Red Light   35
Flight Frenzy   36
The Voluntary Vagabond   37
The Choir Confession   38
The Divine Deal   39
Never Too Late   40
The Jungle Gym   41
Checked Out   42
Aging Gracefully   43
The High School Do-Over   44
Church Clothes   45
Taste of Heaven   46
Dead Ends   47
From Broke to Blessed   48
The Greatest Story Ever Told   49
Game Day Praise   50
The Forgiving Galaxy   51
Fitness, Forks, and Faith   52
Treasure of the Soul   53

Clean Dramatic Monologues

Clean Dramatic Monologues   54

Where's Dash?   55
Wrongfully Accused   56
Sleepless Nights   57

A New Spark   58

The Ring I Didn't Want   59

Facing the Lift   60

Stopped in My Tracks   61

The Truth Revealed   62

Second Opinion   63

The Longest Spelling Bee Ever   64

On the Scene   65

The Heat of the Case   66

Not in My Classroom   67

Ripple Effect   68

Party of Two   69

Moment of Truth   70

Worth the Wait   71

The Price of Kindness   72

Shape Up or Ship Out   73

Don't Walk Away   74

Pull Your Weight   75

I Said Yes   76

Big Break   77

Saved by a Cat   78

The Weight of the Cape   79

Clean Comedic Monologues

    80

Mother-in-Law's Big Moment   81

Eyes on the Prize   82

The Pageant Fiasco   83

When Hunger Strikes   84

The Art of Overthinking   85

The Way to His Heart   86

The Prom Patrol   87

The Black Friday Game Plan   88

Love and Allergies   89

Night Owl   90

Baby on Board   91

Tall Tales   92

The Professional Complainer   93

The Potluck Predicament   94

Diagnosis Everything   95

Dad Rules   96

Drivers Ed   97

Grocery Store Code of   98

Conduct Fame Looks Good on   99

Me Stand Down Comedy   100

Teatime   101

Sedated   102

Hands Off My Lunch Runaway   103

Fail   104

The Cheapest Dad Ever   105

Conclusion   106

Appendix   107

About the Author   109

Introduction

Welcome to Clean Cuts: Volume 1, the first in a series of carefully curated monologue collections designed to help you refine your craft while staying true to your values. Whether you're an actor preparing for an audition, rehearsing a new role, or seeking material to strengthen your performance skills, this book offers a variety of pieces that are both family-friendly and faith-inspired.

But Clean Cuts isn't just for actors, it's also for those who love to read captivating stories. These monologues are written to entertain, inspire, and connect, making them just as enjoyable to read as they are to perform.

In this first volume, you will find monologues on a wide range of themes, hope, redemption, personal growth, and lighthearted moments. suitable for audiences of all ages.

While some of these pieces are faith-based and rooted in Christian themes of spirituality and reflection, others focus on the universal emotions of love, humor, and the complexities of human relationships. Each piece is carefully written to avoid profanity, suggestive content, or anything inappropriate, allowing you to engage with characters and stories that align with your values.

These monologues can also be adjusted to fit your performance needs, whether by shortening a piece for time, adapting the gender, or making minor modifications to align with a specific character or setting.

Whether you're preparing for a role in film, TV, or on the stage, Clean Cuts: Volume 1 offers material that will help you sharpen your skills, stay true to your integrity, and connect with the heart of your performance. These monologues are designed to challenge you as an actor while providing a platform to showcase your talent with authenticity and purpose.

Through this first volume, I hope you will find inspiration, deepen your connection to the craft of acting, and ultimately, shine in every role you take on.

Faith-Based Dramatic Monologues

A Miracle on the Doorstep

Synopsis: A person recently saved by faith struggles with the devastating discovery of an eviction notice. Wrestling with doubt, they recall a scripture that leads them to prayer; and a miraculous answer. (Approx. 90 seconds)

No. No, no, no... this can't be real.

Eviction notice.

How? I've been doing everything right! I gave my life to You, God. I walked away from drinking, got a job, and cleaned myself up. I've been trying so hard... and now this?
I wanted to show my kids the new me that I'm not the broken mess I used to be. But how can they visit me now? Where am I supposed to take them?

And I don't even get paid for two more weeks! What am I supposed to do until then? I thought You were supposed to make a way! I thought... I thought life was supposed to get better with You in it!

(Stops, deep in thought, the temptation of alcohol crossing their mind.)

No. I'm not going back to that. I won't. One drink won't fix this. One drink won't make this pain go away.

What was it the preacher said last Sunday? Ahh... "Do not be anxious about anything, but in every situation, by prayer and petition, with thanksgiving, present your requests to God."

God, I need You. I'm scared. I feel like everything is falling apart, and I don't know what to do. Please, Lord, make a way. Help my unbelief. Show me that You're here.

(Spots an envelope nearby and picks it up.)

"God put it on my heart to bless you. He sees you, and He loves you."

(Tears falling, looking upward with gratitude.)

Thank You, God. Thank You.

The Right Thing

Synopsis: Sitting in their car after finding a wallet in an empty parking lot, a person is tempted to keep the money inside. Faced with the weight of their convictions, they choose to do what's right. (Approx. 90 seconds)

A wallet. Just lying there in the parking lot.

And this... This is a lot of money.

Nobody saw me pick it up. Nobody even knows I have it.

I could really use this money. The holidays are coming up, and the kids have been through so much. They deserve something this year: a real Christmas, not me scraping by and making excuses again.

This could solve so many problems. Rent. Groceries. Maybe even pay down that bill I've been avoiding.

(Looks at license)

A suit? Of course. The guy is probably loaded. Probably doesn't even need this. He won't even miss it.

I can't... I mean, that's not right. I know it's not right.

But...It's not like it's stealing if I found it, right? Maybe this is one of those "blessings in disguise" moments. God, is this You answering my prayers?

No. No, that's not You. You wouldn't give me something by taking it from someone else.

This guy has a name. A face. Probably a family. What if this is his Christmas money? What if he's got his own bills to pay?

God, I've asked You to provide, and You always do. It's not always how I want, but You've never let me down. Keeping this? That's not who I am.

I don't know what will happen next. But I trust You will take care of me.

(Picks up the phone, dialing.)

Hi... I found a wallet, and I'd like to turn it in.

Melting Faith

Synopsis: A person reflects on how a simple moment with ice cream taught them about God's timing and trust in His plan. (Approx. 1 minute)

You ever notice how fast ice cream melts? One second, it's perfect, and the next, it's dripping all over your hands, making a mess. I used to be like that; so impatient.

Always rushing, grabbing, trying to make life happen on my terms.

There was this one time as a kid I begged my mom for ice cream. She said, "Not yet." But I couldn't wait. I snuck into the freezer, grabbed a bowl, and ate it so fast I didn't even taste it. Then the brain freeze hit me, and the mess... oh, it was everywhere.

I remember her walking in, shaking her head. She didn't yell. She just said, "If you'd waited, I was going to make sundaes for us both."

And that's me with God sometimes. Grabbing at things He's already promised me, too impatient to wait. I get ahead of Him, thinking I know better, and end up making a mess of everything.

But God... He's patient. He doesn't yell. He just waits for me to come back to Him, sticky hands and all, and says, "If you'd waited, I had something so much better for you."

Now, I'm learning to be patient. To trust God's timing. Because when it's His way, it's not just ice cream; it's the entire sundae.

Riding the Storm

Synopsis: A person recounts a vivid dream about surviving tornadoes and finding peace at an amusement park. While sharing the dream, they reflect on its meaning, trying to seek God's purpose in it. (Approx. 90 seconds)

I had the craziest dream last night. I was in the car with my family, and it was storming. pouring rain, thunder, everything. We could barely see the road, but we kept going. It felt like the storm would never end.

And then, out of nowhere, it just... stopped. No rain. No wind. Just this eerie silence. I got out of the car, and when I looked around, I saw these tornadoes. Four of them. Huge funnels spinning on each side of me.

One by one, they spun off into the distance: north, south, east, and west. One was so close I thought for sure it was going to hit us. But it didn't. Not one of them touched us.
And then, just like that, they were gone.

The sun came out, and it was beautiful. I was at an amusement park right by the beach. I could hear the waves and kids laughing, and it felt so peaceful.

I've been thinking about it all day. What does it mean? Is God trying to tell me something? The tornadoes felt like everything I've been carrying: stress, fear, all these things I can't control. And yet... they didn't touch me. Is He reminding me that He's in control, even when life feels chaotic?

And that ending... maybe it's His way of showing me that no matter how wild the storm gets, He's leading me to something better. That there's peace on the other side if I just keep trusting Him.

I know you've been dealing with a lot lately, too. Maybe this dream wasn't just for me. Maybe it's for both of us. To remind us that God is with us, no matter what it looks like.

(Takes a deep breath)

We have to trust Him. There's a blessing on the other side of the storm. I know it.

I'm Here, Dad

Synopsis: A child visits their estranged father, unconscious in the ICU, and pours out years of regret, anger, and love. As the situation takes a turn, their raw emotions reach a breaking point. (Approx. 90 seconds)

I... I don't even know where to start. It's been years. Years, Dad.

I told myself I wouldn't be the first to reach out. It was your job, wasn't it? You were the parent. You were supposed to fix it. But God... He kept nudging me over and over. "Call him." "Write him." "Go see him." And I didn't listen. I ignored Him because I was stubborn: because I thought it was your responsibility to make the first move.

And now here you are. In this bed. Unconscious. And I'm standing here wondering if I've waited too long.

Do you even know how much I missed you? How many times I picked up the phone and then put it back down? How many times I told myself, "No. He should call me first."?

Why didn't you? Why couldn't you? Did you even care about me at all?

I told myself I didn't need you. That I could move on without you. But I lied to myself, Dad. I needed you. I still need you.

I'm sorry. I'm sorry for not listening to God sooner. I'm sorry for letting my pride get in the way. I forgive you, Dad. For everything. And I hope... I hope you can forgive me too.

(Suddenly, a loud beeping noise fills the room.)

What's happening?

What's going on? Someone, someone help him!

I love you, Dad! I love you!

Don't leave me!

Rising from the Rubble

Synopsis: A mayor addresses a devastated town after a natural disaster, calling for unity and faith in God amidst the challenges they face. (Approx. 90 seconds)

(Standing on a makeshift stage, looking out at a weary crowd.)

Ladies and gentlemen, neighbors, friends...

This past week, our town has faced devastation like we've never seen before. The floodwaters didn't just wash away homes; they swept through our hearts and our hopes. The roads are gone, and the power is out. Businesses, schools, everything we thought was unshakable has been shaken.

But do you know what hasn't been swept away? Us. We're still here. Bruised, yes. Broken, maybe. But here.

Now, some people told me to keep this speech focused. "Stick to resources. Talk about rebuilding." And believe me, we'll do all of that. Help is coming. We'll rebuild, one brick, one beam at a time. But bricks and beams won't heal this town, not on their own.

I was also told, "Don't talk about God. This isn't the time for that." Well, I say there's no better time for God than when we're standing in the ruins, trying to figure out how to rise again. Because if we're going to rebuild, we need more than supplies; we need faith.

Look around you. We've lost so much, but we haven't lost each other. And we haven't lost Him. God is still here. I see Him in the neighbors sharing what little food they have left. I see Him in the volunteers pulling strangers out of the wreckage. I see Him in every single one of you, showing up despite your own pain to help someone else.

This isn't about differences, disagreements, or divisions. This is about what unites us: our humanity, our compassion, and our faith.

Let's be the hands and feet of Jesus to one another. Let's rebuild this town, not just physically but spiritually. Let's show the world that when disaster strikes, love, and faith shine brighter than any storm.

We are not just a town. We are a testimony. A testimony that with faith, unity, and God's strength, even the greatest storms cannot break us.

Thank you.

Grandma's Recipe

Synopsis: A grandchild prepares their late grandmother's famous coconut pie for Thanksgiving. As they teach someone the recipe, they reflect on their grandmother's faith, love, and wisdom. A missing egg brings an emotional breakdown, but they ultimately find comfort in the lessons their grandmother taught them. (Approx. 90 seconds)

(Standing in the kitchen, stirring a bowl, speaking to someone nearby.)

Alright, so Grandma always said the key to her coconut pie wasn't just the coconut. "You've got to mix love into it, baby," she'd say. "That's the secret ingredient."

First, you start with the filling. Sweetened condensed milk, sugar, shredded coconut, and just a pinch of salt. Grandma said the salt "balances the sweet, just like God gives us strength in the hard times."

Oh, and don't forget the vanilla. Not too much, though. Grandma always gave me the side-eye when I got heavy-handed. She'd say, "Baby, that's not pie, that's dessert soup!"

It's hard, isn't it? First Thanksgiving without her. I keep thinking she'll walk through that door, wearing her apron, humming "How Great Thou Art."

She always told me, "Baby, life is like this pie. God takes the broken pieces, the messy parts, and turns them into something beautiful. But you must trust Him to bake it just right."

Anyway, now we add the eggs. Wait. Where are the eggs?

No, no, no... I thought I had everything!

I just wanted to make it perfect, you know? For her. For everyone. But now... now I can't even do that.

She's gone. She's really gone. No more hugs. No more "I'm proud of you, baby." No more... pie lessons.

But she wouldn't want me to fall apart over an egg. She'd say, "Baby, don't you dare let one thing stop you. Hold on to God. He'll give you what you need."

Grandma was right. Life's not about getting it perfect. It's about showing up, trying, and trusting God to fill in the gaps: just like He always does.

I'm Tired of This

Synopsis: A frustrated individual storms into their home after being cut off in traffic, venting to someone about the exhaustion of always being the bigger person. As they process their emotions, they realize that staying kind and faithful is worth it, no matter how draining it feels. (Approx. 90 seconds)

(Storming into the house)

I'm so tired of this!

You wouldn't believe what just happened. I was driving; minding my own business, in my lane: when this car came out of nowhere, cut me off, and nearly sideswiped me. I slammed on my brakes, and do you think they even cared? No! They had the nerve to yell and honk at me like I did something wrong!

I'm done. I really am. Every single day, it's something. I try to do the right thing, open doors for people, smile, say "hello," let people cut me in line; and what do I get? Nothing. No "thank you," no acknowledgment. Just a world full of people who think kindness is weakness.

And don't even get me started on how they treat Christians. People assume we're soft. They say things like, "Oh, they'll just turn the other cheek." Well, what if I don't want to? What if I'm tired of turning the other cheek? What if I'm tired of always being the bigger person?

I know, I know. You don't have to say it.

I know what the Word says. "Do not grow weary in doing good." I know that. And I know I shouldn't let this stuff get to me. But sometimes... sometimes it feels like too much. Like I'm just pouring out and pouring out, and no one is pouring into me.

But then I think about Him. I think about how many times God has been patient with me, how many times I've messed up and taken His grace for granted, and He still blesses me anyway.

That's why I do it. Not because people deserve it, because, let's face it, they don't. I don't. But God does. He sees it. His Word says, "We will reap a harvest if we do not give up." That's what I'm holding on to. That it'll all be worth it one day.

Forgiving the Unforgivable

Synopsis: A grieving parent takes the stand in court during the sentencing of a drunk driver who killed their child. Beginning with grief and anger, they ultimately choose forgiveness, finding healing through faith. (Approx. 120 seconds)

Your Honor, thank you for allowing me to speak today.

I've spent a lot of time thinking about what I would say if I got this chance. To be honest, I wasn't sure if I could do it. Nothing I say here today will bring my child back. Nothing will undo the pain. But I need to speak. I need to say this.

You took my child. My baby. They had their whole life ahead of them: dreams, plans, a future. And now... now there's nothing. Just silence where their laughter used to be. Just emptiness and pain.

You made a choice that night. You got behind the wheel, knowing you'd been drinking. And because of that choice, my child is gone. I'm left to pick up the pieces of a life shattered by your selfishness.

Do you know what it's like to bury your own child? To see their lifeless body and know they'll never smile again? Never graduate, never get married, never grow old?

I wanted to hate you. Oh, I did. I wanted to scream, to curse your name, to see you suffer like I have. Because what you did is unforgivable.

But then I realized... the hate wasn't hurting you. It was only hurting me. It was chaining me to this pain, to this anger, to this grief. And I couldn't live like that anymore.

I'm a follower of Jesus Christ, and He commands us to forgive. Not because it's easy, not because the other person deserves it, but because forgiveness sets us free.

Most people couldn't forgive what you've done. And honestly, I wouldn't blame them. But this forgiveness isn't for you; it's for me. It's for my child. It's for the peace I need to move forward.

I forgive you. Not because what you did was okay, because it never will be. Not because I've forgotten; because I never will. But because I refuse to let your choices define the rest of my life.

And I pray that one day you'll feel the full weight of what you've done. That you'll turn to God and that His grace will change you the way it's changed me.

Thank you, Your Honor.

This Is Our Moment

Synopsis: A football coach delivers an impassioned pre-game speech before the championship, inspiring the team with themes of unity, perseverance, and faith. (Approx. 90 seconds)

Men, this is it. Everything we've worked for, all the blood, sweat, and sacrifice has led us to this moment.

But tonight? It's not just about a trophy. It's about something bigger. It's about this team. This family. The bond we've built through every practice, every challenge, every time we got back up when the odds were against us.

You've already proven you belong here. But now it's time to finish what we started. The other team? They're good. But they don't have what we have. They don't have the heart that beats in this room, the fire that's fueled by hard work, perseverance, and grit.

When you step out on that field, I don't care about the crowd, the scouts, or the other guys lined up against you. I care about how you play for the man beside you. You fight for him, just like he'll fight for you.

And when it gets tough; and it will: you dig deep. You trust the work you've put in. You trust each other. And you trust God because He's with us tonight, just like He's been with us every step of the way.

So, play with heart. Play with intensity. Play like everything is on the line. And when the final whistle blows, you'll know you left it all out there and you gave it everything you had.

Now get out there and show them who we are. Let's bring it home.

Is She the One?

Synopsis: A single man tells his friend about a woman at work he's interested in. He admires her beauty, confidence, and faith while wrestling with the nerves of making the first move. Ultimately, he decides to trust God and go for it. (Approx. 90 seconds)

I saw her again today. In the break room.

She's beautiful, man. Her eyes are just gorgeous. And her smile? It's the kind of smile that lights up the room. She's smart and confident; the total package.

We spoke briefly today. It was just a "hi, how are you doing?" kind of thing, but I felt something there. I don't know; it was the way she said it, like she actually cared.

Then the other day, I overheard her talking about church. She was saying how much her faith means to her, and that just hit me. It's not every day you meet someone who's beautiful and loves God. That's rare, and it's... honestly, it's attractive.

Now, I'm trying to figure out what to do. I know it's on me: I'm the man. I'm supposed to make the first move. But I keep thinking, "What if she's just nice to everyone? What if I ask her out, and she says no?"

But then again... what if she's interested in me too?

I've been praying about it, asking God for some clarity. Because, honestly, I'm ready to find my wife. I don't want to waste time on something that isn't going anywhere.

You know what, bro? I'm going to ask her out right now. If it's God's will, it'll work out.

I've got this!

Always a Bridesmaid

Synopsis: A woman tries on her bridesmaid's dress for a friend's wedding and reflects on her longing for love and her faith in God. As she wrestles with being "always a bridesmaid, never a bride," she finds hope in trusting God's timing for her own story.
(Approx. 90 seconds)

(Standing in front of a mirror, smoothing the fabric of her bridesmaid's dress.)

Oh. It's pretty. And it fits nicely too.

(Turns slightly, checking the back in the mirror.)

Another wedding. Another dress. This is my fifth time. Five weddings, five dresses, five times standing at the altar for someone else. Always a bridesmaid, never a bride.
I'm happy for her. I really am. She deserves this. She deserves to be celebrated. But... when is it my turn?

I mean, I've been patient. I've prayed. I've waited. And every single time, I tell myself, "It'll happen when it's supposed to." But sometimes... sometimes, it feels like God's forgotten me.

No. No, He hasn't forgotten about me. I know He hasn't. Maybe... just maybe, I've been focusing on the wrong thing in this season. Maybe instead of worrying about what I don't have, I should be loving myself more. Getting closer to God. Trusting that He's working on me for what's ahead.

This dress? It's not the one I've been dreaming about. But I know one day when it's my time, I'll wear the dress meant for me, standing at the altar with the man of God He's prepared just for me. And when that day comes, it'll be perfect because it'll be His plan, His timing, His blessing.

Alright. Time to celebrate.

Breaking the Cycle

Synopsis: A person shares their story during an alcohol recovery meeting about how they fell into alcoholism after their mother's passing, the generational pain that fueled their addiction, and how a stranger's kindness and faith helped them find hope, recovery, and purpose in Christ. (Approx. 120 seconds)

Thank you for letting me share my story.

It started when my mom passed away. She was my everything. Losing her felt like the world fell apart. My dad couldn't handle it either; he turned to drinking to numb the pain. I guess I thought if it worked for him, it would work for me too.

It didn't.

Drinking didn't just dull the pain; it buried me in it. I kept telling myself I had it under control, but the truth was, it had control of me. Things spiraled fast. I lost my job, my home, my hope.

I was homeless, wandering the streets, thinking this was just how my story was going to end. And then, seemingly from nowhere, someone showed up. A stranger. They were Christian. I didn't want to hear about God or faith, but they didn't just preach at me; they gave me a meal. They saw me and talked to me like I was still human.

They kept coming back. Checking on me. Praying for me. One day, they handed me a Bible. I didn't think much of it at the time, but something about their kindness, it stuck with me.

Eventually, I couldn't take it anymore. I decided to get cleaned up. That stranger connected me with their church, and the church introduced me to a recovery program.

For the first time in years, I felt hope again.

I got a job. I started showing up for life instead of hiding from it, and most importantly, I found Jesus.

Now, I don't just want to stay sober, I want to help others find the way out too. I know what it's like to feel hopeless, to think you're too far gone. But I also know what it's like to be found.

If God can save me, He can save you too. And I'm here to help you see that.

The First Day

Synopsis: On the first day of school, a teacher stands in an empty classroom, practicing their welcome speech for the students. They reflect on the challenges some students face, their calling as a teacher, and their faith. Though prayer isn't allowed in schools, they take a moment to pray privately for their classroom, the students, and the year ahead. (Approx. 90 seconds)

(Standing at the front of the classroom, practicing their welcome speech.)

Good morning, class. Welcome to a new school year! I'm so excited to be your teacher. This year, my biggest expectation is simple: respect. Respect for each other, for yourself, and for this classroom. This is a place to learn, to grow, and, yes, to make mistakes. Mistakes are just part of the process.

(Pauses.)

Okay, that sounds good.

But it's not just about what I say, is it? Some of them are going to come in here already carrying more than they should. Broken homes. Tough neighborhoods. Struggles that make focusing on school the last thing on their minds.

How do I reach them? How do I get through to the kid who's hungry, or angry, or scared? They need more than lessons and grades. They need to know someone's in their corner.

I know prayer isn't allowed in schools anymore. But that doesn't mean I can't pray for them right now.

God, I lift up this classroom, every single student who's about to walk through that door. You know their stories, their struggles, their dreams. Give me the wisdom to teach them, the patience to guide them, and the heart to love them like You do. Bless this school year, Lord. Protect this room, this school, these kids. Help me to be what they need. In Jesus' name. Amen.

Alright. I'm ready.

(Students start walking in.)

Good morning! Come on in and find your seat.

Honoring God's Call

Synopsis: A person sits across from their boss, explaining their decision to resign. They share how the job no longer aligns with their Christian values, and though they don't know what's next, they are trusting God's plan for their future. (Approx. 60 seconds)

I wanted to sit down with you personally to say this: I'm resigning.

This hasn't been an easy decision. I've appreciated the opportunities I've had here, and I've learned so much. But lately, I've been feeling a strong conviction that I can't keep ignoring.

This job... it no longer aligns with my values. As a Christian, my faith is a big part of who I am, and I've found myself in situations where I feel like I'm compromising that.

I've prayed about it a lot. Honestly, walking away from something stable like this is scary, especially when I don't know what's next. But I trust that this is the right step, even if it's not the easiest one.

Thank you for understanding and for everything I've gained during my time here.

A Brother's Goodbye

Synopsis: A deeply emotional farewell as an older sibling says goodbye to their younger brother, Ezra, who is heading off to college. They share heartfelt advice, memories, and their unshakable love, reminding him to put God first and never forget his worth. (Approx. 120 seconds)

So... this is it, huh? You're really leaving.

Ezra, I'm so proud of you. You worked so hard for this, and you deserve every bit of what's coming next. But... I won't lie; this is hard. You've always been my little brother, my partner in crime, my shadow. And now, you're off to start this whole new chapter of your life without me.

I'm going to miss you, Ez. I'm going to miss hearing you laugh at the dumbest jokes. I'm going to miss how you always leave your shoes in the middle of the hallway, no matter how many times I tell you not to. I'm even going to miss the way you steal my food when you think I'm not looking.

But more than anything, I'm going to miss having you around because you're not just my brother. You're my best friend.

Listen, before you go, there are some things I need you to hear. First, don't ever forget who you are. God made you special. You've got this strength in you, this light that people can't help but notice. Hold onto that. Don't let the world dim it.

Second, don't forget where you came from. Mom and Dad worked so hard to give us the life we have. And they've raised you to be kind, humble, and faithful. Carry that with you wherever you go.

And last but not least, keep God at the center of your life. College is going to be full of distractions, full of moments where you feel lost or unsure. When that happens, pray. Lean on God. He won't let you down.

Ezra... I'm so proud of you. I'm excited for you. But I'm also selfish enough to say I'm going to miss you like crazy. The house isn't going to feel the same without you.

You're going to do great things. I know it. And no matter how far you go, I'll always be here. I'm your biggest fan, your biggest supporter. And I love you more than words can say.

Now, go make us proud, little brother.

Behind the Mask

Synopsis: An actress confronts her sister Michelle, who is concerned about her health and eating habits. Initially annoyed, the actress breaks down, revealing her struggles with anorexia, self-worth, and the pressures of her career. Faith and hope emerge as she begins to face her reality. (Approx. 75 seconds)

Mind your business, Michelle! Seriously. Why are you always in my face about this?

I eat. I'm fine. Can you just stop? I don't need a lecture, okay? I've got it under control.

Do you know what it's like to stand in front of a camera, knowing millions of people are going to see you and judge you? To hear them whispering, "She's put on weight." "She's not as pretty in person."

I'm doing what I have to do. This is my career. My life. If I'm not perfect, I'm nothing. Do you think I like starving myself? That I like hiding behind layers of makeup because I can't stand what I see?

(Tears falling.)

I used to believe I was fearfully and wonderfully made like the Bible says. But now? Now, all I see are flaws. I feel ugly. It's like the world has convinced me I'll never be beautiful enough, no matter how hard I try.

I try to pray. I try to trust God. But it's hard when the world screams the opposite at me every single day.

Maybe you're right. Maybe I do need help. But how do I even start?

I want to believe God can fix what's broken in me. I want to believe I'm more than this.

Michelle, will you pray for me? I don't want to live like this anymore.

The Right Bait

Synopsis: While fishing with children at a pond, a character shares a story about catching their biggest fish after learning to use the right bait. The story takes a heartwarming turn as they connect the lesson to how Jesus calls us to be fishers of men, encouraging the children to share the gospel with love, no matter their age. (Approx. 75 seconds)

Let me tell you about the biggest fish I ever caught. It was right here at a pond, just like this one. I'd been fishing for hours, no bites, not even a little tug. I was frustrated, ready to pack it up and call it a day.

Then Grandpa came over, took one look at my line, and said, "You're using the wrong bait." I thought he was joking. But he handed me a different lure, showed me how to use it, and said, "Try again."

So, I cast my line with that new bait, and before I could blink: bam! I caught the biggest, most beautiful bass I'd ever seen. I couldn't believe it. And you know what? After that, I kept catching fish, one after another.

Grandpa wasn't just teaching me how to catch fish that day. He was teaching me something bigger. You see, Jesus calls us to be fishers of men, to share His love with the world. But just like fishing, we need the right bait. And that bait? It's love, kindness, and patience.

When we show people who Jesus is by how we treat them, by being kind, forgiving, and caring, they'll see something different in us. They'll see His love. It doesn't matter how old you are; even you kids can do this.

So, remember, whether you're fishing for bass or for people's hearts, the right bait makes all the difference. And don't forget, there's always room for one more on Jesus' boat.

Alright, kiddos, let's see who's going to catch the biggest fish today!

Strength in Weakness

Synopsis: A person wrestles with an unbearable toothache while confessing their fear of going to the dentist. Through reflection, they realize the pain is a reminder of their need to trust God's strength instead of their own. (Approx. 75 seconds)

My tooth hurts so badly. I didn't sleep a wink last night. Even drinking water sends this sharp, shooting pain all the way to my head.

And don't tell me to go to the dentist. I know, okay? But the thought of sitting in that chair, hearing those drills, the needles... I can't. The last time I went, it was awful. I told myself I'd never go again.

I've tried everything to fix it on my own. Saltwater rinses, clove oil; anything to dull the pain. Last night, I even slept on my Bible, hoping God would just take it away. And for a moment, it worked. The pain eased, and I thought, "Maybe I can get through this without going." But by morning, it was back, worse than ever.

You know, it hit me today: isn't this how life feels sometimes? We go through pain, we try to avoid it, fix it, make it stop on our own. But pain has this way of reminding us that we can't do it alone. That we need God.

There's a verse that says, "Where I am weak, He is strong." I think that's what I need to hold onto right now. Because it's not just about this tooth. It's about letting go of my fear and trusting Him to give me strength when I don't have it.

I know I need to go. I know sitting here, afraid, isn't going to fix anything. But God's brought me through tougher things than this. I can do this.

I'll go call the dentist now.

The Crumb Snatcher

Synopsis: During Thanksgiving dinner, a person reflects on how a dog scavenging for crumbs reminded them of a biblical story. They draw a heartfelt connection between faith, gratitude, and eagerly seeking God's word. (Approx. 90 seconds)

(Sitting at the dinner table, glancing down at Sasha staring intently at their plate.)

Sasha, you are something else. First, you're under the table snatching every crumb, and now you're over here, staring at me like I owe you something. You've already eaten!

Watching you today reminded me of a story in the Bible; the one where the woman tells Jesus, "Even the dogs eat the crumbs that fall from the master's table." I never really understood that story before, but looking at you, Sasha, I think I finally do.

Crumbs are enough. You don't care if it's a crumb or a feast, you're determined to get it, aren't you, girl? And that's how we should be with God.

You know what, family? On this Thanksgiving, when we're surrounded by so much food and so many blessings, I realize how often I take it all for granted. Even a crumb of God's goodness is more than enough. Just one word from Him can change everything.

And here I am, with a plate full of blessings, forgetting to be grateful sometimes. But Sasha? She's down here acting like every crumb is a treasure.

I want to be like that. Hungry for every bit of God's word, every blessing He has for me. If just a crumb can satisfy, imagine what the whole feast could do.

Alright, girl. Come here. You've earned this.

(Hands Sasha a piece of food.)

Until We Meet Again

Synopsis: A parent with a terminal illness shares final words with their children. They reflect on the extra time God granted despite prayers for a different outcome, urging them not to lose faith. (Approx. 90 seconds)

Children... come closer. Let me see your faces one more time. We prayed for a miracle, wholeheartedly believing God would heal me completely. It's just not the outcome we expected.

But do you remember what the doctors said? They said I wouldn't last the summer. Yet here I am, talking to you months beyond that. I lasted longer than anyone expected, and I believe that's because our prayers weren't ignored. God answered them, just not in the way we imagined.

The Bible says, "He has made everything beautiful in its time." For a while, I struggled with that verse. Why couldn't my time be longer? Why couldn't I be healed the way we pictured? But every extra day has been a gift. We laughed together, cried together... I got to hold you a little longer.

Don't give up on God just because my healing looks different than we wanted. Don't think your prayers went unheard. By giving me these extra months, God granted us precious moments we wouldn't have had otherwise.

I've made mistakes, but teaching you about Jesus and doing my best to show you His love was never one of them. Promise me you'll keep seeking after God. Keep sharing His word because the world needs hope, and Jesus is our living hope.

I wish I could stay with you a little longer, but I'm at peace, knowing I'll be with God. I love you more than words can say... and I always will.

Reflection of Faith

Synopsis: A woman recites affirmations to rebuild her confidence but is triggered by the sight of her scars, leading to a raw moment of doubt and a transformative encounter with God. (Approx. 90 seconds)

I am smart. I am strong. I am caring. I am beautiful. Beautiful... right?

Who am I kidding? Every time I walk outside, people stare. They whisper. I can feel it, even when I pretend I can't.

I am strong. Strong? If I were strong, why does it still hurt? Why does their laughter echo in my mind? Why do I feel so... small? Weak?

God, why? Why did You let this happen to me? I... I trusted You. I was obeying your word, wasn't I? So why the accident? Why the scars? Do You even care how hard this is? How hard it is to look in the mirror and... and see this staring back at me?

I can't even say these words without doubting them. How am I supposed to believe them? How, God?

But... You do see me, don't You? Even when I can't see myself. You're the one who made me.

You knew me before I was even born. And these scars? These scars don't scare You. You're not ashamed of me. You've never turned away, even when I've turned away from You.

Maybe... maybe You're not done with me yet. Maybe these scars aren't the end of my story.

Maybe it's just a chapter.

I am beautiful. Because You made me. I am strong. Because You give me strength. I am enough. Because I am Yours.

I am beautiful. I am strong. I am enough. And I believe it.

The Finish Line

Synopsis: A coach encourages a discouraged track runner who wants to quit. The coach sees the runner's potential and uses scripture to inspire them to believe in themselves and keep going. (Approx. 90 seconds)

Look at me. Hey, I said, look at me. I know this is hard. Believe me, I've been there. Life's not easy, and sometimes, yeah, it's easier to just throw in the towel and walk away. But you can't. Not now, not ever.

You've got something special in you, something God put there for a reason. And yeah, running this race, it's not always going to feel good. It's going to burn, it's going to hurt, and some days, it'll feel like you just can't go on. But that's when it matters most.

You know, there's something about running a race that's just like life. It's not about how fast you go or how easy it feels. It's about keeping your eyes on what's ahead, staying steady, and not giving up, no matter how much you want to. I see the way you doubt yourself, the way you let those negative thoughts get in your head. But let me tell you something: those voices? They don't know you like I do. They don't see your strength, your potential. And they sure don't know the plans God has for you. Plans to make you thrive, to give you hope and a future.

It's okay to feel weak sometimes. It's okay to feel like you can't take another step. But don't let that stop you. Don't let the pain, the fear, the doubt win. Because you're stronger than you think. And you've got someone bigger than all this who's running right alongside you.

So, what do you say? Are you going to let this moment define you, or are you going to dig deep, take a breath, and push forward? Not just for the race, but for you. For the life waiting on the other side of this.

You've got this. I believe in you. And more importantly, God believes in you. So, get up, brush yourself off, and win this race!

A Heart Set Apart

Synopsis: A heartfelt breakup monologue where the speaker explains their decision to end a relationship to honor their commitment to God. They express love and patience for their partner while emphasizing the need to live a life aligned with their faith. (Approx. 75 seconds)

I've been thinking about this moment for a while now, and it's breaking my heart to even say the words out loud. But I can't keep living this way. Not anymore. I've given my life to Christ, and I'm trying to live in a way that honors Him. That means I can't keep doing the things we've been doing. The drugs, the drunken nights, the recklessness; it's just not who I am anymore.

I invited you to church, but you didn't want to go. And that's okay: I'm not judging you. I know God loves you, and He's patient, but I've realized we're not on the same page. The Bible talks about being equally yoked, about walking together with someone who's going in the same direction. Right now, we're not.

This isn't easy, and it's not because I don't care about you. I do; so much. That's why this hurts so badly. But loving you doesn't mean I can stay in this. Loving God means I must trust Him, even if it's hard. I'm far from perfect, and I've made so many mistakes, but God has forgiven me, and He can do the same for you. When you are ready, He will be there with open arms.

Take care of yourself, okay? I'll be praying for you. Goodbye, my love.

Don't Jump

Synopsis: A stranger spots someone about to jump off a bridge and urgently intervenes, sharing their own experience with a suicide attempt and the power of God's love to encourage the person to choose life. (Approx. 120 seconds)

Stop! Don't do it! Please, just... just listen to me for a second. You don't know me, and I don't know you, but I've been where you are. I know what it feels like to think there's no way out.

A few years ago, I thought I couldn't go on. I was drowning in pain, convinced the world would be better off without me. So, I took a bottle of pills. I thought it would end everything, but it didn't. I woke up in a hospital bed, and I'll never forget the look on my mom's face. She wasn't angry: she was devastated. That was the moment I realized that my pain didn't just affect me. It rippled out to everyone who loved me.

I know it feels unbearable right now, like this pain will never end. But it does. It gets better. God... He saved me that day, and He can save you, too. He knows your pain, the nights you cry yourself to sleep, the weight you carry every single day, and He loves you more than you can imagine.

You don't have to carry this alone. Let me help you. Let me show you that there's hope beyond this moment, that the future you can't see yet is worth fighting for.

Please, step back. You were made for more than this. You were made for a purpose. You might not believe that right now, but I do. I'm standing here because I believe in you.

You're not alone. You're loved. And no matter what you've done, no matter how broken you feel, God's love for you has never wavered. Let Him show you what life can be beyond this moment. Please step back. I'm begging you!

That's it. Take my hand. Let's face this together, one step at a time.

Faith-Based Comedic Monologues

Mistaken Generosity

Synopsis: A hilariously awkward encounter unfolds as a person mistakes the mayor for a homeless individual, delivering a heartfelt speech on generosity. It humorously explores the lesson of not judging by appearances while celebrating the importance of being willing to help. (Approx. 90 seconds)

Hi there! Are you doing okay, sir? You look like you could use a little help. Listen, I couldn't just walk by without stopping. Here, take this. It's not much but maybe grab something to eat. Everyone deserves a full stomach, right?

I want you to know God's got you. He doesn't leave anyone behind. Trust me, life gets tough, but a little kindness can go a long way. No shame in that. Here, take it. It's okay. Go ahead. You can have it.

Hold on a minute. Aren't you Mayor Johnson? The actual mayor of this city! I can't believe this! I thought I was having a Good Samaritan moment, and instead, here I am, trying to feed the mayor. So embarrassing!

Well, I guess you don't need my money or my motivational TED Talk. Wait... you're here for the big landscaping reconstruction project, right? I heard all about it on the news. That's why you're dressed like someone who just lost a bet with their lawnmower.

That's incredible, though! It's so great to see a mayor who's hands-on, really leading by example. Honestly, I respect that so much.

But, uh, maybe next time, wear a name tag? Or a shirt that says, 'Undercover Mayor'? Something to avoid moments like this because clearly, I'm not great at context clues.

Anyway, thank you for not laughing; or calling security. Keep the money. Or, I don't know, maybe use it as a donation for your cause? It was a pleasure meeting you, Mayor Johnson. And hey, next time, maybe let me know where I can sign up to help. It's not every day you see a mayor rolling up their sleeves like this!

Mime For a Change

Synopsis: A heartfelt pitch to a partner about quitting a stable job to pursue a surprising passion: becoming a professional mime. This humorous piece explores dreams, self-expression, and God's unexpected plans for our lives. (Approx. 90 seconds)

So, babe, picture this; I've had an epiphany. I'm thinking of quitting my job and becoming a professional mime. Yeah, I know, it's like I'm whispering my dreams to the wind, but hear me out. I've been practicing those invisible box moves in the mirror, and let me tell you, I've got the skills to pay the nonexistent bills.

You remember the last time we were at that carnival, and there was that mime doing the whole trapped-in-an-invisible-box routine? I was mesmerized! It's like, who needs words when you can have an entire conversation with your face?

Now, I know you're thinking, "Why on earth would you quit your job to be a mime?" Well, babe, it's about self-expression, breaking free from the shackles of corporate monotony. Besides, my invisible rope skills are on point.

Okay, I get it, you're worried about stability, bills, and all that practical stuff. But haven't you heard, babe? They say, "Leap, and the invisible safety net will appear." Okay, maybe I made that up, but it sounds good, doesn't it?

Imagine me standing on that imaginary stage, doing my mime thing, and suddenly, a single tear rolls down my cheek. Why, you ask? Because I've found my true calling, and it's beautiful, like a silent masterpiece painted on the canvas of life.

Remember that time we talked about destiny and God's plan? Maybe God wants me to spread joy through mime. Maybe He's saying, "Go forth, my child, and mime your heart out!"

I'm ready to take the plunge into the world of mime, and who knows, this might just be my ticket to a life less ordinary. Plus, imagine the dinner conversations we'd have; "How was your day, dear?" (mime jazz hands and invisible wall gestures) Pure gold, right?

I'm a Glutton

Synopsis: A dramatic yet comedic confession about the realization of being a glutton after hearing a convicting sermon at church, leading to a humorous reflection on buffet indulgence, stress-eating, and the importance of putting God first. (Approx. 90 seconds)

I have a confession to make. I'm a glutton! I know, I know, it sounds dramatic but listen! I went to church today, and for the first time ever, the pastor preached about gluttony. GLUTTONY! Out of all the topics, he had to pick that one. Of course, I'm sitting there thinking somebody must have seen me at the Country Buffet this weekend.

Don't judge me, but I had seven plates. Honestly, after the second one, I wasn't even that hungry, but I was determined to get my $12.99 worth.

That fried chicken, mac and cheese, steak, and shrimp Alfredo? Oh, they were calling my name. And let's not forget the cheesecake and brownies, mm mm mmm. But hey, I had a salad and a Diet Coke too, because it's all about balance, you know.

While sitting in church, the pastor said something that really hit me: gluttony isn't about size; it's about habits. And here I was, thinking gluttony was just a fancy word for overeating at Thanksgiving. Turns out, it doesn't matter how much you weigh, you can still be doing way too much.

And it's not just buffets. When I'm stressed, instead of praying first, I raid the fridge. When I'm overwhelmed, I call on chips and salsa instead of calling on Jesus. I've been treating food like it's the answer to my problems when I should be seeking God first.

But thank God for grace. He doesn't leave us stuck in our mess, whether it's overeating, overthinking, or overindulging in other areas of our lives. I've realized that anything can become an idol if we aren't careful: food, video games, even social media. Instead of finding comfort in those desires, we should make an effort to find comfort in Christ.

So, I'm working on it. Next time, instead of seven plates, I'll stick to two... okay, maybe three if it's Taco Tuesday. Hey, I'm a work in progress. Just pray for me!

Fishing in the Storm

Synopsis: A comedic yet inspiring monologue about a group of friends who go fishing and get caught in an unexpected storm. Filled with humor and biblical reflections on doubt, trust, and God's protection, this story showcases the unpredictable nature of life and faith. (Approx. 120 seconds)

I should have known it was going to be a wild day when Robert showed up with a life jacket over his fishing shirt. He said, "Better safe than sorry," and I laughed: but now I'm thinking Rob might be a prophet.

So, we head out on the boat. It's me, Robert, and a couple of other friends, and we're having the time of our lives. The fish are biting, we're catching so many we're practically running out of room in the cooler. Rob says, "Let's go deeper! The big ones are out there." And because Rob has a way of convincing us to do questionable things, we go deeper.

At first, everything is great. Then... the clouds roll in. Fast. I mean, one minute, it's sunny and peaceful; the next minute, the sky looks like it's auditioning for the Book of Revelation. I'm looking at Rob like, "Did you check the weather?" and he says, "I... uh... prayed about it." Great.

Then the rain starts. Not a sprinkle, oh no. This is a "build an ark" kind of rain. The boat is rocking, water is sloshing everywhere, and Robert decides this is the perfect time to say, "Hey, maybe one of us should try walking on water!" Really, Rob? Now?

Meanwhile, I'm gripping the side of the boat, praying like never before. "Lord, I'll never skip church again if you get us out of this." The waves are getting bigger, and we're all starting to panic. Doubt is creeping in. Will we make it? Did we go too far?

But then I remember the story of Jesus calming the storm. I'm thinking, "If He did it for the disciples, He can do it for us." So, I say out loud, "God, we trust You." And a few moments later, the wind starts to calm down, and the rain eases up. Rob looks at me and says, "Well, remind me to stand next to you during the next thunderstorm!"

By the time we make it back to shore, we're drenched, exhausted, and holding onto that cooler full of fish like it's a trophy. We were so grateful we made it back safely. God protected us through the storm, and He taught us a little something about trust along the way.

So, the moral of the story: if Robert ever invites you fishing, just say no. And if you do go, bring a life jacket, an umbrella, and a prayer warrior. But most importantly, don't forget to trust God... because even when the storm hits, He's in control.

Is He the One?

Synopsis: A woman shares a lighthearted and faith-filled account with her best friend about a surprising moment with a coworker she finds intriguing when he finally asks her out. As she reflects on their interactions, she humorously highlights how God is at the center of it all. (Approx. 120 seconds)

Girl, you are not going to believe this! Remember that guy I mentioned? The one who spoke to me in the break room the other day that was really nice and extremely handsome? Well, it finally happened.

Okay, first of all, let me just say this: God must have taken His time when He made him. Like, seriously, I had to pray for extra focus just so I wouldn't get distracted during my last meeting. "Lord, help me keep my eyes on You and not on this fine man in accounting!"

I've never been one to mix work and romance. I was always told, "Don't get your honey where you make your money." But something about him makes me think he might be worth the exception. He's not flashy or loud, and he's so respectful. I even saw him reading his Bible at his desk the other day. I was like, God, is this a sign?

And let's talk about those glances. Oh, he thinks he's slick, but I've caught him looking at me more times than I can count. I can tell he wants to ask me out, and I smile, but he has to be the one to do it. After all, it is "he who finds a wife finds a good thing," not the other way around.

So, there I am, eating my chicken salad sandwich, minding my business, when he finally comes over. He looks at me and says, "I overheard you talking about church the other day. I'm a Christian too. I think you are absolutely beautiful, and I would love to take you out to dinner sometime?"

I couldn't resist teasing him a little. I said, "So, you finally worked up the courage, huh? I mean, I thought you might be interested, but I wasn't sure. He laughed and said, "Well, I needed to make sure my timing was perfect. It's not every day you ask out someone this amazing." He had me blushing so hard I thought I might turn into a tomato, but I played it cool. I responded with, "Dinner sounds great. And for the record, I've noticed you too."

Girl, I've been praying for someone who loves God and isn't afraid to show it, and I really hope this is God answering that prayer. We're going out to dinner this weekend, and I'm excited to see where this goes. Don't worry, I'll keep you updated, but let's just say I've got a really good feeling about this one.

Making Waves

Synopsis: A comedic and faith-filled monologue about a person's first experience learning to swim. Through awkward moments and biblical reflections, they discover the humor and lessons in trusting God and overcoming fear. (Approx. 75 seconds)

So, guess who finally decided to learn how to swim? Yep, me. And let me tell you, it's been an experience.

I had no idea there were so many rules! "Kick your legs like this," "Move your arms like that," "Don't forget to breathe." Breathe? I thought breathing was supposed to be automatic, not something you had to remember.

Then, there was my instructor. Bless his heart, he's so patient. He kept saying, "Trust the water! It'll hold you up!" Trust the water? I barely trust my own two legs on dry land. But then I remembered what the Bible says about God not giving us a spirit of fear, and I thought, "Okay, God, I'll try; just don't let me embarrass myself too much."

So, I let go of the edge, and the next thing you know, I begin sinking to the bottom of the pool. Arms flailing, lungs burning, and for a split second, I'm thinking, "Is this how I meet King Jesus?" My instructor yanks me up and says, "Great job! You're getting there!" Getting where sir? To the pearly gates?

Each time I get back in the pool, it feels a little less terrifying. It's just like faith. You might start out shaky, but the more you trust God, the more you realize He's been holding you up all along.

Grace at the Red Light

Synopsis: A comedic and faith-based monologue about an unexpected encounter with a police officer after unknowingly running a red light. Through humor, self-reflection, and biblical truth, the character reflects on mercy, grace, and second chances. (Approx. 90 seconds)

So, I get pulled over, and the officer leans in with that classic line, "Do you know why I pulled you over?" And I'm sitting there thinking, "Was it because you saw me and wanted to ask for my number?" Of course, I didn't actually say that out loud. Although the officer was very attractive.

I just sat there staring, trying to act like I had no idea what was going on, because, honestly, I didn't. I was too busy singing along to some worship music to notice anything else. Then it hit me: "Oh no, did I run a red light? Lord, please tell me I didn't run a red light."

Turns out, I ran a red light.

The officer tells me, "You completely disregarded the traffic light." And I'm sitting there, sweating bullets, thinking, "I'm going to jail!" Then reality hits, and I'm like, "Okay, I'm probably just getting a ticket, but my bank account is already hanging on by a thread.

While the officer is running my license, I'm having a little prayer meeting right there in the driver's seat. "Lord, I know I deserve this ticket. I wasn't paying attention. But Your Word says, "Your mercies are new every morning." Could you maybe extend some of that mercy to me this afternoon?"

The cop returned to my car, handed me my license, and said, "I'm letting you off with a warning. Just pay more attention next time."

I almost cried. Isn't that just like God? Giving us what we don't deserve when we least expect it. As I drove off, I laughed and thought, "Next time I have a worship session in the car, I'll keep the volume low enough to focus on both God and the stoplight."

Flight Frenzy

Synopsis: A comedic and faith-based monologue about the chaos of realizing you're late for a flight, featuring a whole family in a mad dash, misplaced items, and a quick prayer that shifts the day. (Approx. 75 seconds)

Oh no. Oh no, oh no, oh no! WE'RE LATE! Everyone, WAKE UP! It's 6:45! The flight is at 8! MOVE!

Why is no one moving? Kids, where are your shoes? Wait; where are MY shoes? Honey, why are you just standing there? No, we do NOT have time for coffee! Grab it to go.

No, you cannot pack the dog! And why are your backpacks empty? You've had weeks to pack for this trip!"

Okay, STOP! Everyone, stop. Let's pray. Lord, we need You right now. We overslept, and everything feels chaotic. Please help us get to the airport on time. And Lord, help me not lose my mind on the way there. Amen.

Alright, back to it! MOVE, people, MOVE! Why are the keys in the fridge? Who even? Never mind, not important! Honey, put down the coffee maker. You're not bringing the coffee maker. Wait... what's this? Looks like a text from the airline: Flight 6899 has been delayed.

Thank You, Jesus! See? God answers prayers. Honey, go ahead and make your coffee. Kids, you've got five minutes to finish packing, and I need to catch my breath because that was intense!

Next time we are setting 3 alarms and packing 6 months in advance!

The Voluntary Vagabond

Synopsis: A homeless individual explains to a reporter why they chose to live without a home, weaving in biblical principles and funny anecdotes. Their unconventional lifestyle turns into an inspiring testament of faith and freedom. (Approx. 90 seconds)

Oh, you want to know why I chose to be homeless? Well, let me tell you; it's not because I couldn't make rent or anything like that. This is on purpose! Yeah, people usually tilt their heads and say, "Why would anyone do that?" I tell them, "Hey, Jesus didn't have a mortgage either." Scripture says, "Foxes have holes, birds of the sky have nests, but the Son of Man has nowhere to lay His head." Boom. Biblical validation.

Listen, I know Aunt Katie probably sees this news clip and starts clutching her pearls, wondering what happened to me. But you know what? I've learned more out here than I ever did in a cubicle. For example, you don't need ten pairs of shoes when you've got faith to walk on water. Okay, I haven't exactly walked on water yet, but last week I stepped over a puddle, and I'm calling it progress.

People ask if it's hard, and sure, there are moments. Like last week, it rained, and my blanket got soaked. But that's when Psalm 23 popped into my head: "He makes me lie down in green pastures." And let me tell you, a soggy sleeping bag in a grassy ditch counts as a green pasture if you squint.

But here's the thing, being homeless has taught me how to trust God for my daily bread. Sometimes literally. Like when I found a perfectly good bagel in the trash. Before you raise an eyebrow, it was still in the wrapper! That was my loaves-and-fishes moment. Okay, it was just me and the bagel, but still.

And let's talk about freedom. You don't realize how much freedom you have until you're not tied down by bills. I can pack up and move whenever God says, "Go!" Okay, sometimes it's less God and more the parking lot security guard telling me, "Move your van," but you get the point.

Look, I know people think I've lost my mind. But the truth is, I've found a better perspective. I don't need a fancy house or a designer sofa. Plus, God promised me a mansion someday. Until then, I'm content knowing that God's got me covered; sometimes by a tarp but still covered.

The Choir Confession

Synopsis: A choir member shows up late to rehearsal and tries to charm their way out of trouble with an elaborate, over-the-top excuse. When the story falls apart, they confess to oversleeping and reflect on their struggle with punctuality, tying it back to faith and growth. (Approx. 90 seconds)

Okay, I know I'm late, but before you get mad, just hear me out! It all started when I was driving here and saw this guy stranded on the side of the road. His car had a flat tire, and I thought, "Well, somebody's gotta help." So, I pull over, but, uh... it turns out I don't actually know how to change a tire. So now we're both just standing there, staring at it like it's a math problem, and he's looking at me like, "So, do you know what you're doing?"

Then, this van pulls up: Praise God, right? Except it's full of Girl Scouts selling cookies. And somehow, I end up buying five boxes of Thin Mints because, apparently, I can't say no to a ten-year-old with a sash. So now I'm standing there, holding cookies, the guy still has a flat tire, and I'm thinking, "I am so late."

And as I was leaving, the gas light came on. I'm like, "Are you serious right now?" So, I pull into the nearest gas station, but the only pump available seems to barely work. I'm standing there, tapping my foot, praying for patience, thinking, "Lord, this rehearsal is looking further and further away."

... You're not buying this, are you?

Okay, okay. I'll tell you the truth. I overslept. I decided to take a quick nap, telling myself, "Just a few minutes, and I'll get up in plenty of time!" But then my brain was like, "Five more minutes won't hurt." Next thing I know, it's thirty minutes later, and I'm flying out the door to make it to rehearsal on time.

I know I need to do better. This isn't the first time. I've set multiple alarms, and somehow, I still manage to snooze through them all. I've even labeled them things like, "GET UP NOW" and "YOU HAVE NO EXCUSE," but apparently, I can ignore even myself.

I apologize for being late. I know it's inconsiderate. I want to show up, not just physically, but with intention. Psalm 90:12 says, "Teach us to number our days, that we may get us a heart of wisdom." For me, that means valuing time and being where I'm supposed to be when I'm supposed to be there. But I'm here now, and I'm ready to sing, on key and everything.

I appreciate you being so understanding.

The Divine Deal

Synopsis: A car salesman pitches a great car to a pastor, using humor and sincerity to connect while respecting the weight of the decision. They emphasize the car's value for ministry and daily life, balancing comedy with reverence. (Approx. 75 seconds)

Pastor Luis, I have to tell you, this car right here isn't just any car; it's practically a ministry on wheels. Dependable, spacious, and it's the kind of car that'll turn heads for all the right reasons.

Let's talk details. The engine? Runs smoother than your worship team on Easter Sunday. It's powerful and steady, ready to take you wherever you're called.

The AC is ice cold; it'll keep you cool after you bring the heat from the pulpit.

And the tires? Built to handle highways, back roads, and even the occasional gravel parking lot at those outdoor tent revivals. And the trunk? It's got enough space for sound equipment, groceries for the food pantry, and luggage for when you surprise your wife with a well-deserved vacation.

But here's the thing: I'm not just trying to make a sale. I want you to feel confident in your choice. This car is reliable, and I believe it could really serve you well.

Let's take her for a spin. If you're still unsure, pray about it. If this is the car for you, you'll know. And if it's not, that's okay. I'm confident we'll find the perfect car that meets your needs and serves your mission.

Never Too Late

Synopsis: A witty Grandmother humorously shares their journey of going back to school to get their GED, reflecting on faith, perseverance, and the humor of being the oldest student in the room. (Approx. 120 seconds)

Well, I never thought I'd be sitting in a classroom at my age. The last time I held a pencil this much, Eisenhower was president. But here I am, back to get my GED, proving it's never too late to learn. Or at least that's what my grandkids said when they signed me up for this.

Let me tell you, these classes are no joke. Can you believe math has letters in it now? Back in my day, the only letters I worried about were on the report card. And don't even get me started on technology. They handed me a tablet, and I said, "I already took mine this morning. It's for my arthritis." Turns out, they meant the fancy computer kind.

But you know what? This whole experience has taught me something about faith. You've got to believe in what you can't see, like how I passed that algebra test. I walked in praying, "Jesus take the wheel," and somehow walked out with a passing grade. God is good.

The young folks in my class keep calling me 'Grandma,' but I don't mind. I just tell them, 'Grandma's here to show you how it's done.' I might move a little slower than them, but I've got something they don't, patience and a lifetime of figuring things out. Plus, I bring snacks. You'd be amazed at how far cookies can go when you're trying to make friends.

I've learned that it's not about how old you are but how willing you are to show up and keep trying, even when the odds feel stacked against you. Philippians 4:13 says, "I can do all things through Christ which strengthens me." And let me tell you, I've been leaning on that verse like it's the handrail on a steep staircase.

So, here's to the cap and gown comeback. Watch out, world, because this grandma's getting her diploma. And if I can do it, you can, too. Just don't ask me to help with your math homework.

The Jungle Gym

Synopsis: A frustrated gym-goer vents about the madness of New Year's resolution season. Packed parking lots, overcrowded machines, and the inevitable decline of attendance come spring all make for a funny yet introspective reflection that points back to Christ's consistency. (Approx. 90 seconds)

You won't believe what happened at the gym today. I pulled into the parking lot, and I'm not kidding, it looked like they were giving away free memberships or something. Every spot was taken! I had to park so far away; I felt like I got my cardio in just walking to the door.

And when I finally got inside? Forget it. Every machine was taken. The treadmills? Full. The weights? Gone. I even saw someone sitting on a bench. not working out; just texting! And I thought, "Lord, grant me the strength not to flick a resistance band in their direction."

Here's the thing: it's January. We all know what that means. New Year, new me! Right? Everyone's fired up and ready to hit their goals, and I love the enthusiasm I do. But we also know how this plays out. By March, half of these people will be back at home, eating snacks and watching TV, and I'll finally be able to use the leg press without waiting in line like it's the DMV.

And I get it. Commitment is hard. It's easier to start something than it is to stick with it. But this whole gym madness got me thinking about my walk with Christ. How often do we treat our faith like a New Year's resolution? We're all in at first: reading the Bible every day, praying for hours... and then life gets busy. The enthusiasm fades. But here's the difference: Christ doesn't quit on us. He's not just there when it's convenient or when things feel easy. He's consistent even when we're not.

You know what? Maybe I'm taking this whole thing too seriously. At the end of the day, it's just a treadmill. I'll survive. And hey, worst case scenario, I can count walking back to my car as my workout for the day.

Checked Out

Synopsis: A grocery store clerk vents about the quirks and frustrations of dealing with customers, only to reflect on the rise of self-checkout and the possible loss of her role. Through faith, she realizes the value of human connection, even in the most annoying moments. (Approx. 120 seconds)

Ms. Barbara, I've got to tell you, you always brighten my day when you come through my line. Working here at the grocery store is always an adventure. Like yesterday, this guy asked me, "Do you have organic water?" Organic water? I almost told him, "Sure, it's in aisle five, right next to the dehydrated rainbows." But I bit my tongue and just smiled.

And don't even get me started on the people who roll in five minutes before closing. They've got carts so full you'd think they're opening their own grocery store. And, of course, they want to pay in exact change... after digging through every pocket and purse. Meanwhile, I'm just standing here, trying to keep my face holy and not roll my eyes too hard.

You know what really gets me? Self-checkout. At first, I thought, "Great, less work for me!" But then I realized those machines don't need a paycheck or lunch breaks, and now, every time I look over at the self-checkout, I notice there are fewer of us cashiers on the floor. Honestly, it's got me wondering if my job is next. I mean, how do you compete with a robot that doesn't need bathroom breaks?

But here's the thing... as much as I joke about it, I've realized something. It's not just about scanning groceries or asking paper or plastic. It's about people. Like that mom who comes in overwhelmed with three kids hanging off the cart, and I bag her groceries extra carefully because I know she's had a day. Or the older gentleman who cracks a joke every time he buys his bananas. Those moments? They don't happen at self-checkout.

The Bible says, "Whatever you do, work heartily, as for the Lord and not for men." This job might not be glamorous, and self-checkout may be the future, but I'll take the quirks and flaws of real people over a lifeless machine any day.

Truth be told, Ms. Barbara, some days I want to quit. But then someone like you comes through my line, and I remember, this job may not be perfect, but it's perfect for me. Besides, where else could I work where someone actually believes "organic water" exists?

Aging Gracefully

Synopsis: A funny and heartfelt reflection on the challenges of aging, from dodging roller coasters to rethinking basketball while finding strength in faith and humor. (Approx. 90 seconds)

Aging is not for the faint of heart. I used to think people were joking when they said, "Wait until you hit your 40s." They laughed. I shrugged. And now? Now I'm the one laughing... but only to keep from crying.

Take roller coasters, for example. Remember when we used to ride those things back-to-back, screaming our lungs out like it was nothing? Well, I tried to relive my glory days last week. I got on one of those big, twisty upside-down ones and thought, "This is going to be amazing!" By the first drop, I was screaming, "Lord, what have I done!" And by the second loop, I was praying for the ride operator to have mercy and hit the emergency stop.

And basketball? Forget about it. Back in the day, I could shoot hoops for hours. Now, if I try to play, I'm out there wheezing like a tea kettle after two minutes. The other day, a kid asked me if I needed a break. A kid! I told him, "I'm not tired, I'm just... pacing myself." Meanwhile, my knees were screaming for an ice pack.

It's not just the big stuff, either. Even small things are different. I bent down to tie my shoe this morning and had to think about it first. Like, I actually paused and asked myself, "Is this even worth it?" Then the other day, I sneezed, and my back gave out. Can you believe that? A sneeze!

Ecclesiastes 3:1 says, "For everything there is a season, and a time for every purpose under heaven." I'm starting to realize that just because I'm not doing all the things I used to doesn't mean I'm missing out. This season? It's teaching me patience. It's teaching me to listen to my body and, more importantly, to lean on God. Because let's be real, I might not be as fast, strong, or flexible as I used to be, but His strength is made perfect in my weakness.

So, I'm okay if I don't ride roller coasters or play basketball like I used to. I'm more than happy to sip lemonade and cheer everyone on from the sidelines.

The High School Do-Over

Synopsis: A comedic reflection on a recurring dream about going back to high school to finish missing credits. The monologue explores the absurdity of the dream while weaving in subtle faith-based insights. (Approx. 90 seconds)

I keep having this recurring dream that I'm back in high school. Not as a cool guest speaker or someone inspiring the next generation. Oh no. I'm there as a full-time student, trying to finish the credits I apparently "missed." Like, excuse me? I graduated! I have a diploma in a box somewhere, probably next to my old yearbooks and prom pictures.

The dream always starts out normal too. I'm walking down the hall, trying to remember my locker combination, and then out of the blue, the principal: who I've never seen a day in my life says, "You're missing a half-credit of gym and two credits of algebra." Gym? Algebra? I'm lucky if I can touch my toes and count to 10 at the same time these days.

And the other students? They're all teenagers, looking at me like I'm a substitute teacher who got lost on the way to class. I'm just over here just trying to blend in with my backpack and a lunchbox that somehow has my name written on it in Sharpie. Then I start to think, why am I in high school with a Tickle Me Elmo lunch box?

The funniest part? In the dream, I'm super worried about my grades. Like, I'm sitting in chemistry class, trying to figure out the periodic table, and thinking, "Lord, how did I ever pass this the first time?" And somewhere between trying to memorize the quadratic formula and dodging dodgeballs in gym class, it hits me: this has to be a message from God. Maybe it's about unfinished business, or it's His way of reminding me to pay attention. Either way, I'm waking up in a cold sweat, thanking God for the revelations... and for not making me actually go back.

Christ is the ultimate teacher, and His class is the only one I'm signing up for these days. His lessons may not come with homework or gym uniforms, but He gives us the wisdom and grace we need to pass the test. And as for high school? That's staying right where it belongs. in my dreams.

Church Clothes

Synopsis: After being told by an overzealous usher to "wear church clothes," the speaker vents to a friend about the baffling interaction. Humor and scripture combine to reflect on modesty, judgment, and what truly matters in worship. (Approx. 120 seconds)

Let me tell you about what just happened. I visited a church today that wasn't too far from my house. I walked in feeling good, ready to worship, right? Modest outfit, nothing too flashy; nice blouse, a knee-length skirt, and flats. Then here comes this usher, stopping me at the door like she's TSA. She leans in, real serious, and whispers, 'Next time, you might want to consider wearing church clothes.'

Church clothes? Excuse me, but did I miss the launch of the church clothes section at Macy's? Because I've checked, and unless it's between cookware and clearance shoes, I haven't seen it! And what exactly are church clothes supposed to look like? A ball gown? A choir robe?

Look, I wasn't out here in yoga pants or a crop top that says Blessed but Not Stressed, okay? I was modest. My knees were covered, my shoulders were covered, and there wasn't a single rhinestone or sequin in sight! And you know I love sequins. It's like she expected me to show up looking like Sister Mary Clarence from Sister Act.

Don't get me wrong; I respect the house of God. I love being in His presence. But I'm pretty sure Jesus isn't up there going, "Hmm, Lisa wore flats instead of heels today. Erase her name from the Book of Life!" That's not the Savior I know.

That's the reason some people don't go to church now. They're scared they'll be judged for what they're wearing when they're just seeking after God. How many people have been turned away because someone decided they didn't look the part?

I politely told her, 'You know, the Bible says in 1 Samuel 16:7, "Man looks at the outward appearance, but God looks at the heart." She looked at me as if she was surprised I even knew the scripture. Then she had the audacity to say, 'Well, you should still dress up for church.' As if my clothes determine the quality of my worship!

We've got to be mindful of how we treat people. If someone shows up to church, it means they're looking for God, and that should be what we celebrate.

So next week, I'm showing up in whatever lets me praise freely; even if it's sneakers. And if she tries to stop me again, I'll just smile and say, 'Oh, these are my church clothes.'

Taste of Heaven

Synopsis: A competitive participant shares their hilarious, larger-than-life perspective on the church fundraiser cooking competition. Fueled by confidence, humor, and a love for Jesus, they aim to win big for both the Lord and themselves. (Approx. 90 seconds)

Alright, let's just get this out of the way: I'm here to win. Yes, it's for a good cause, but let's not pretend this isn't a competition. And between you and me, I've got this in the bag. Not to brag: but okay, let's brag a little; I've been training for this my whole life. Some people are called to preach or sing. Me? I was called to cook.

Look at my setup. Everything is perfectly prepped, my ingredients are fresher than manna from heaven, and my knives? Sharper than a Pharisee's tongue. Meanwhile, did you see Brother Kevin's station? He's a great guy and all, but that man can't even boil water.

Now, let me tell you about my dish. Lemon garlic chicken with rosemary. Simple, elegant, divine. And, of course, I asked the Lord to bless it. The seasoning isn't just salt and pepper; it's got a little faith, a lot of love, and just enough cayenne to make your taste buds shout hallelujah. I'm not saying it's the best thing you'll ever eat, but... okay, yes, I am. It's the best.

Sister Carol keeps going on and on about her 'famous' macaroni and cheese. And it's good, I'll give her that. But famous? I mean, come on. Adding breadcrumbs on top doesn't make it revolutionary.

You know what sets me apart, though? It's not just the food. It's the calling. 1 Corinthians 10:31 says, 'Whatever you do, do all for the glory of God.' That includes this chicken. I'm not just cooking; This is my ministry. I'm just out here using my gifts for His glory... and maybe for a tiny bit of bragging rights.

So, judges, I hope you're ready. One bite of this chicken, and you'll know who the winner is. But don't just take my word for it, take a bite and experience a taste of heaven on earth.

Dead Ends

Synopsis: A hilarious recount of a hair salon trip gone wrong, where a trim turned into a dramatic cut. The speaker humorously reflects on the spiritual parallels of cutting to grow and trusting the process with a biblical twist. (Approx. 120 seconds)

She cut my hair! I walked into that salon thinking I was about to leave with a fresh, bouncy look. you know, just a little off the ends. Nothing crazy. I told her, 'I would like a nice trim.' And she nodded, all calm and professional like she understood. Why do they always act like they understand, only to come for your whole life with those scissors?!

I'm sitting there, scrolling on my phone, quietly checking my emails, and I look up... and my hair is on the floor. Like, all of it. I said, 'Excuse me, what part of TRIM did you misunderstand?'

I looked in the mirror and barely recognized myself. I walked in looking like I could star in a shampoo commercial and walked out looking like I was joining the army of the Lord. I had to ask God to calm me down and bridle my tongue because I was about to say some things that might need forgiveness later!

She kept saying, 'It'll grow back! Healthier! Better!' Oh, now she's a prophetess, I guess. Let me tell you, I was too angry to hear any of that. I just kept staring at the floor like, 'Is that really my hair down there?'

But then, as I sat there holding back tears, it hit me. Sometimes, we hold onto dead ends because we think length means strength, but it couldn't be further from the truth. Just because it's long doesn't mean it's healthy. Split ends are sneaky; they look fine at first, but before you know it, they're messing up everything else. You're thinking, 'It's not that bad,' but if you'd just let go of the dead weight, your hair: or your life. could be so much stronger and healthier.

Sometimes, you've gotta trust the process and let go, even if it feels like too much in the moment.

So yeah, I went in for a trim and came out looking like G.I. Jane. But maybe that's what I needed. A fresh start. And if God can work all things for good, maybe He can even use a haircut to teach me something. I'll just be over here deep-conditioning and praying for growth and patience along the way.

From Broke to Blessed

Synopsis: A faith-filled journey from growing up poor to living in abundance, with reflections on God's provision, hard-earned lessons, and the joy of never forgetting where you came from. (Approx. 120 seconds)

Growing up, we were so broke that we didn't just pinch pennies; we put them in a chokehold! I mean, our idea of 'fine dining' was turning ramen noodles into spaghetti. Add a little ketchup and some prayer, and voila: Italian night! And let's not even talk about cereal. If we had milk, it was a holiday. And when the milk ran out, you better believe we used water. I still have trust issues with Cocoa Puffs to this day because of that.

And clothes? Y'all, I was the original 'Thrift Hunter' before it was cool. Mom always said, 'Why buy new when we can make it unique?' In other words, we shopped exclusively from the clearance rack and then tailored everything with duct tape and determination.

But here's the thing: even though we didn't have much, we had joy. Our parents constantly reminded us, 'The Lord will provide.' And I'd think, 'Great, but can He provide some name-brand Pop-Tarts just once?' But you know what? They were right. God always came through. Sometimes, it was a neighbor dropping off groceries, and other times, it was finding a $5 bill in an old jacket. Either way, He showed up.

Fast forward to today, and let's just say water cereal isn't on my menu anymore. God has blessed me abundantly, and I'm so grateful. But I'll be honest: there are moments when I catch myself acting a little bougie. Like, I'll complain if my almond milk isn't the 'unsweetened vanilla' kind. Meanwhile, the younger me is shaking my head, saying, 'We drank water with sugar and called it a treat. Go sit down somewhere.'

But here's the real lesson: God can take you from broke to blessed, but you've got to trust Him.

Even when we had little to nothing, we had God: and that was enough. So now, whether I'm eating filet mignon or dollar-menu nuggets, I know who my Provider is.

So, if you're in a season of struggle, remember this: God's not just providing; He's preparing you. And one day, you'll look back and laugh, not because it was easy, but because He was faithful.

The Greatest Story Ever Told

Synopsis: Excitement about an amazing movie leads to a realization about the importance of sharing the gospel with the same passion, offering humor and inspiration. (Approx. 90 seconds)

Oh, my goodness! Let me tell you about this movie I just saw. It was incredible! I laughed, I cried, I cheered. At one point, I gasped so loud that the person next to me gave me the side-eye. Usually, I'm all for good theater etiquette, but this movie was so good I threw all of that out the window.

You HAVE to see it; I've been telling everyone! My neighbors? Told them. The mailman? Oh, I definitely told him. The lady at the grocery store? I showed her the trailer. And don't even get me started on social media. I posted about it three times already.

Let me just say this, if you haven't seen it yet, you're missing out. It's got everything: twists, turns, that one perfect song at just the right moment. It was the best movie I've seen in a long time.

Wow... I just realized something. I'm out here evangelizing for a movie like I'm on the marketing team. I've told twenty people about this film in two days, shared it online, and practically begged folks to watch it. But when's the last time I put this much energy into telling someone about Jesus? Ouch.

I mean, think about it. If you love something, you share it, right? You don't keep it to yourself. If you find a new show, a great restaurant, or the perfect pair of shoes, you're telling the whole world about it. So why not the gospel? It's the best story ever told; and besides, it's not just a story. It's the truth. If I can hype up a movie this much, I can also share about the Savior of the world.

Game Day Praise

Synopsis: A frustrated yet funny worship leader hilariously compares the enthusiasm of cheering at ball games to the silence during worship. (Approx. 90 seconds)

Alright, can we talk for a second? I noticed something funny. Last night at the game, you all were bringing the house down. I saw the footage: cheering, jumping, and losing your minds over a home run. Now, don't get me wrong, I love that energy! But then we come into worship, it's like everyone's waiting for an elevator. Hands tucked away, barely a hum.

Now, I'm not saying we need fireworks and confetti in worship, although that would be memorable: but if you can shout for a team that doesn't even know your name, why not get loud for the One who calls you by name? Jesus didn't sacrifice everything so we could whisper our way through worship like we're afraid someone's listening.

And hey, don't tell me you're not 'the expressive type.' I saw some of you doing the wave last night at the game. If we can do that, surely, we can lift a hand or two during worship.

And don't make the excuse that you can't sing either. I heard you belting out 'Take Me Out to the Ball Game' during the seventh-inning stretch!

Psalm 100 says, 'Make a joyful noise unto the Lord, all the earth!' That's not a suggestion: that's a heavenly game plan! So don't hold back. Heaven's going to be full of celebration, and I want us to be ready. So, let's step up to the plate and magnify Jesus, the One who gave us the victory.

The Forgiving Galaxy

Synopsis: A faith-based sci-fi comedy set in outer space, combining a humorous alien encounter with themes of forgiveness and grace. (Approx. 120 seconds)

"So, there I am, floating in zero gravity, exploring the stars, when this alien pops out of thin air.

I'm not talking about the cute, big-eyed kind you see on posters; no, this one had three heads, glowing tentacles, and a smell that could knock out a space station. I panicked. I did what any rational astronaut would do, I screamed and threw my snack pouch at it. Turns out, aliens were not fans of dehydrated mac and cheese.

It just stared at me, all three heads blinking, and said, 'Why do Earthlings overreact? We come in peace.' And I'm like, 'You couldn't have sent an email first?' But then, it got awkward. Turns out, this alien wasn't here to invade or abduct, it was here to apologize. Apparently, its species accidentally sent the asteroid that wiped out the dinosaurs. Honestly, though, maybe that was for the best. I mean, can you imagine humans trying to co-exist with T-Rexes? That's a reality show I'm not ready for.

At first, I wanted to be mad. For goodness' sake, they ended a whole era. But then I thought, forgiveness is about letting go and moving on. If God can handle all my slip-ups, who am I to hold a grudge against a glowing tentacle creature?

So, I told it, 'You know what? I forgive you. But maybe double-check your aim next time.' And you know what it did? It hugged me. His three heads, eight tentacles, and that unforgettable smell made for quite the experience. But as I floated there in a slimy embrace, I realized something: forgiveness might be messy, but it's worth it. Even in outer space.

So now, here I am, floating through the galaxy, wondering if I just made friends with the most accident-prone species in the universe. But hey, if God's grace can stretch from Earth to the heavens. I guess it can stretch to aliens too.

Fitness, Forks, and Faith

Synopsis: A hilarious prayer about weight loss turns into a heartfelt realization about perseverance, consistency, and discipline through faith. (Approx. 120 seconds)

Lord, we need to talk. You know I love you, but this weight loss journey? It's testing me. I've tried everything. Keto, paleo, intermittent fasting: even that one where you eat like a caveman. I'm pretty sure cavemen didn't have to resist donuts. And don't even get me started on that juice cleanse. Three days of drinking green liquid that tasted like grass clippings, and for what?

To lose two pounds and gain it back the second I sniffed a cheeseburger? And the gadgets! Lord, I had the best intentions, I went out and bought all the equipment.

Resistance bands, ankle weights, dumbbells, and even one of those fancy treadmills with built-in Bluetooth. I had big plans! But instead of using it, my treadmill is holding my laundry, and my resistance bands haven't resisted a thing. The only workout I've been consistent with? Fork-to-mouth. I mean, at least I'm disciplined in that, right?

Lord, you parted the Red Sea, gave sight to the blind, and made manna fall from heaven. I'm asking you now for a miracle. Your Word says you give and take away, so could you please take away these love handles? Please.

I've been so caught up in the number on the scale that I've ignored the weight I'm carrying in my spirit. Discipline, perseverance, and consistency? Lord, those aren't necessarily my spiritual gifts.

But I get it now. This isn't about shortcuts; it's about the journey. So, help me out here. Give me the strength to say no to late-night ice cream and yes to early-morning walks. Remind me that my body is your temple, even if this temple is currently under construction.

I trust you, Lord. One step, one prayer, one salad at a time. Amen.

Treasure of the Soul

Synopsis: A pirate captures a prisoner for their gold but has a surprising change of heart. Through humor and reflection, the pirate realizes the greatest treasure is faith. (Approx. 120 seconds)

"Arrr, matey! So ye thought ye could outsmart ol' Captain Ashbeard, eh? Look at ye, sittin' there all tied up like yesterday's fishin' bait. Now, I know what yer thinkin'. 'Why's this pirate talkin' instead of makin' off with me gold?' Truth be told, I'm not exactly known for me high moral standards.

As I was eyein' yer shiny loot, somethin' caught me eye: pictures of yer family. And somethin' strange happened, somethin' that's never happened to ol' Captain Ashbeard before: I felt bad.

Like, really bad. Almost as bad as the time I tried to make seaweed stew for the crew. But there it was, right in front o' me; a family countin' on ye to come back safe.

And then, right next to the pictures, I saw somethin' else: a Bible. Now, I ain't the religious type, never have been. But curiosity got the best o' me, so I cracked it open. Wouldn't ye know, the first thing I saw was a scripture about not layin' up treasures on earth where moth and rust destroy but layin' up treasures in heaven. Here I was, tryin' to steal gold, when there's a greater treasure I've been ignorin' me whole life.

I've done some questionable things in me time, things that'd make even the saltiest sailor blush. But outright damagin' me soul for a few shiny coins? Even a scallywag like me has to draw the line.

Don't get me wrong, yer gold is temptin'. But I've learned somethin' in all me years on the high seas: the greatest treasure ain't found in a chest.

So, here's what's gonna happen. I'm gonna untie ye, and ye're gonna take yer gold and go. But let this be a lesson: next time ye're in a bind, don't rely on yer gold. Call on the Captain of yer soul. Now, off with ye! And don't make me regret this! Arrr, and Amen!"

Clean Dramatic Monologues

Where's Dash?

Synopsis: While frantically searching for Dash, the dog they were dog-sitting, someone explains to a friend how they accidentally left the gate open. Desperate and financially struggling, they share their fears about losing their job and their determination to find Dash. (Approx. 90 seconds)

Dash! Dash, come here, boy!

Thank you so much for helping me. I'm a nervous wreck! It's my fault, when I grabbed the mail, I must've left the gate open. I thought I latched it, but I guess not. Now Dash is out here somewhere, living his best life, and I'm about to lose mine.

Dash! I really needed this gig. Things are tight right now; like "counting change for gas" tight, and if I lose Dash, I'm done. Who's going to hire the person who lost their dog? "Hi, I can't even keep a gate closed, but trust me with your pets!" Yeah, right.

Maybe he went toward the park? Or the neighbor's yard? They have rabbits, and Dash loves rabbits. Dash!

What if he went toward the street? Oh no, I can't even think about that. They trusted me, and now their sweet little puppy is... Dash! Where are you!?

I'll check the park. Maybe he's under that big oak tree he likes. Or, oh, he could've followed that food truck that parks on Second Street. You know Dash loves their pup cups.

Dash! Come on, buddy! I'll buy you all the treats you want if you just come back. Please, Dash. I have to find you!

Wrongfully Accused

Synopsis: A person sitting in a jail cell for a crime they didn't commit, opens up to their cellmate about how they ended up being accused of stealing a car. They explain the misunderstanding, their frustration, and their hope for freedom with an upcoming court case. (Approx. 90 seconds)

I shouldn't be in here. I didn't steal that car. I didn't even touch it. I was just walking home, keeping to myself, when my phone slipped out of my hand. It fell right in front of this fancy-looking BMW. All I did was bend down to pick it up. Next thing I know, someone's screaming, "He's trying to steal my car!"

I froze. What are you even supposed to do in a moment like that? I turned around, hands up, trying to explain, but they didn't care. They just kept spewing out accusations. The cops showed up so fast as if they were already looking for someone to pin this on. And guess who was standing there, phone in hand, looking "suspicious"?

They slapped cuffs on me before I could even finish saying, "This is a mistake." Nobody wanted to hear that. They had their story: I was some random person out to steal a car, and that was it. End of discussion. No witnesses, no evidence, just someone pointing a finger and me standing in the wrong place at the wrong time.

And now I'm stuck here, sitting in this cell, waiting for my day in court. I'm hoping that somebody, anybody, will listen to the truth. I've got a lawyer. She says I'm going to win and that justice will prevail. But honestly, it's hard to feel hopeful in here. Every second goes by, and the walls feel like they're closing in.

I just want my life back. That's all. I didn't do anything wrong! I know I've got to hold on to hope. Because if I don't, what else do I have?

Sleepless Nights

Synopsis: A person struggles with insomnia following their mother's death. They share how the sleeplessness is affecting their family, work, and their own sense of self and how they desperately want to heal. (Approx. 90 seconds)

I'm so tired. It feels like every part of me is shutting down, piece by piece, and I can't stop it. I haven't slept since she died. I've tried everything. Working out until I'm exhausted, drinking teas, changing my routine. Nothing works. The second I lay down, my mind starts running in circles, and I can't stop it.

I thought I could push through, that it would get better. But it hasn't. My family needs me, but I'm so worn down that I don't even know how to be there for them. My kids don't ask me to play anymore because I'm either too tired or too irritable. And my spouse? I can see the disappointment. I'm not who I used to be, and it's breaking me.

At work, I'm missing deadlines and snapping at people. This isn't me. I hate it, but I don't know what else to do.

And it all comes back to her. My mom. I miss her so much.

Why did she have to leave me? I keep reaching for the phone to call her, to hear her voice, to ask her what to do. But she's not here. She's never going to be here again. I don't know how to keep going without my mom. It's too much. It's just too much.

I need help. I need to sleep. Please... tell me what to do.

A New Spark

Synopsis: A person shares with their new neighbor how a small kitchen fire in their apartment led to an unjust eviction. Despite the challenges, they reflect on how the ordeal became the push they needed to move forward and purchase their first home. (Approx. 90 seconds)

Why did I move here? That's a good question. Well... I didn't plan on it, that's for sure. It all started with a stupid accident; a grease fire. I was cooking dinner, turned away for a second to grab some salt, and when I turned back, the flames were already climbing. I called the fire department right away. They came, put it out, and the damage was minor. Nobody was hurt.

But my landlord? No compassion. None.

I thought paying for insurance, including fire insurance, meant I'd be covered. But no. They said I was a liability. Gave me 30 days to pack up and leave. I tried to reason with them. I begged. I explained it was an accident, that it could happen to anyone. They didn't care. I'd lived there for five years and never missed rent once, but they still made me feel like I didn't belong.

I was angry. No... I was devastated. All I could think was, "Why is this happening to me? But then... something shifted. I realized that maybe this wasn't the end. Maybe this was my chance to start over.

So, I started looking at houses: not because I was ready, but because I had to. And then I found this place. The moment I walked in, I felt it. This could be home; my home. No landlord breathing down my neck over every little thing. No one to hold something over my head. Just me, owning something for the first time in my life.

Do I wish it had happened differently? Sure. But truthfully? That fire was the spark I needed. It burned away everything that was holding me back. And now I'm here, in this neighborhood, starting fresh. So, yeah, it was a bad situation, but it turned out to be exactly what I needed. Funny how life works like that, isn't it?

The Ring I Didn't Want

Synopsis: A woman confides in her best friend about discovering an engagement ring while helping her boyfriend recover from surgery. She shares her inner conflict about staying with him out of guilt versus following her heart and choosing herself. (Approx. 90 seconds)

Girl, you won't believe what I just saw! I came straight here because I needed to talk to you. I was at his place, you know, bringing him meals, cleaning up a bit, just trying to help him while he's recovering. Then I opened a drawer, and there it was... a ring. A diamond engagement ring. I thought I was imagining things at first, but it was real.

My heart stopped. But it wasn't excitement or happiness that hit me: it was guilt. Crushing, suffocating guilt. Because I don't want to marry him. I know I can't. And now, I have no idea how to even begin dealing with this.

You remember I was going to end things before the accident, right? I had it all figured out: what I'd say, how I'd say it. And then he got hurt, and I couldn't go through with it. I couldn't leave him like that. Who does that? So, I stayed. I told myself I'd stick it out until things settled down. But now... the ring? It changes everything.

He deserves someone who looks at that ring and feels pure joy, not someone who is unsure. He deserves someone who wants to be there, who's excited about forever with him. And that's not me. I care about him so much, but that's not love, right? Not the kind you're supposed to build a life on.

I feel terrible. But I know I can't keep pretending. I've spent my entire life being what other people needed me to be. But what about what I need? When do I get to choose myself? I've gotta tell him. I just... I don't know how. How do I do this without breaking him even more? How do I walk away knowing it'll hurt him so badly? What would you do?

Facing the Lift

Synopsis: A person recounts facing their fear of elevators, believing it was stuck, and finding the courage to overcome their phobia. (Approx. 120 seconds)

I've avoided elevators for years. Years. I'd rather climb fifteen flights of stairs than step into one of those metal boxes. But today... today I decided, enough is enough. I can't let this fear control me anymore.

So, I stepped inside. My heart was pounding so loud I thought everyone could hear it. The doors closed, and it felt like I was locking myself in a cage. I tried to breathe, tried to focus on the buttons, the walls... anything to distract me from my claustrophobic thoughts.

And then it happened. The elevator stopped. The lights flickered for half a second, and I lost it. My chest got tight, and my head was spinning. I grabbed the railing and said, "I can't do this. I'm scared of elevators." The strangers in there with me just stared. I couldn't tell if they felt bad or just thought I was crazy.

My voice was shaky, but I managed to get out, "I can't breathe." One of them said, "It's okay. We're fine. It'll move in a second." But how could they know? What if the cables snapped? What if we were stuck here for hours? What if...? My mind wouldn't stop.

Then the doors opened. Just like that. A man stepped on, holding a coffee like it was just another day. Turns out, the elevator had stopped because he pressed the button from the outside. It wasn't stuck. It never was.

I laughed, but it wasn't because it was funny. It was relief. Embarrassment. Everything all at once. I wanted to shrink into the floor. But you know what? I stayed on. I rode it all the way to my floor. And when the doors opened, I stepped out like I owned the place.

I'm not saying I'm cured. I'm still shaking. But I got on. I faced it. And next time, I'll face it again. Because I'm done letting fear decide where I can and can't go.

Stopped in My Tracks

Synopsis: A person pleads with their boss to keep their job after being late again due to an unexpected train delay. They take accountability for their past tardiness while explaining their efforts to improve and the uncontrollable situation that left them stuck. (Approx. 90 seconds)

I know I'm late again, and I know what you said about this being my last chance. But please, just let me explain. I did everything right today. I got up early, I left with plenty of time, and I was ready to prove that I could do better. But then, the train happened.

I was literally the next car in line to cross when the bells started ringing. The train came, and I thought, "Okay, it'll pass in a minute." But it didn't. It just stopped right there on the tracks. Completely stopped. I couldn't move forward because of the gate, and I couldn't back up because there were cars behind me. I was trapped.

I even took pictures. You can see it, this massive train just sitting there, not moving. I even tried calling the office to let someone know what was going on, but no one answered. I sat there for 20 minutes, watching the clock, knowing I was going to be late again and knowing how it would look.

I get it. I know I've been late before, and that's on me. I own that. I've been working hard to fix it, and today was supposed to be my reset. But this? This was completely out of my hands. I truly did everything I could to be here on time.

I'm begging you: please don't fire me. I need this job, and I've been trying so hard to show that I can be better. I'll do everything I can to prove that I'm worth keeping. Just give me one more chance. Please.

The Truth Revealed

Synopsis: A person confesses to lying about having a college degree while speaking to the HR representative at their new company. They explain why they lied, their family struggles, and how they regret the decision despite their skills and experience. (Approx. 90 seconds)

I know you're probably upset, and you have every right to be. I lied. It's there on my resume, clear as day. I said I had a degree when I didn't. And now you've found out. I wish I could undo it, but I can't. What I can do is tell you the truth.

I was in my junior year of college when my dad walked out on us. Just up and left. My mom was working two jobs, barely keeping us afloat. So, I quit school. I got a job to help keep the lights on, to make sure my little brother didn't have to go to bed hungry. College became the last thing on my mind.

As the years went on, I kept working, moving up, and proving myself. But every time I applied for a new job, the same question came up: "Do you have a degree?" And I panicked. I thought if I was honest, no one would give me a chance. So, I added that one line: a lie. And I've been carrying it ever since.

I know that doesn't make it right. I know I betrayed your trust before I even started here. But please, understand; I'm a good person. I've worked hard to be where I am. I've earned the skills and experience I bring to the table, even if my path wasn't traditional.

I'm sorry. I truly am. And I'll accept whatever decision you make. I just wanted to give you an explanation and help you understand where I'm coming from.

Second Opinion

Synopsis: A doctor delivers life-changing news to a patient, informing them that their second opinion tests reveal a benign growth and no signs of cancer. They explain the results with kindness and professionalism while encouraging lifestyle changes. (Approx. 90 seconds)

I know this past week has been incredibly hard for you. When you first came to me, you were understandably scared: anyone would be after hearing news like that. But I'm so glad you decided to get a second opinion. It's not always easy to question a diagnosis, but it's so important.

After reviewing all your scans, your X-rays, and running additional tests, I can confidently tell you this: you do not have cancer. The growth we saw is benign. There is absolutely no sign of malignancy anywhere. You're cancer-free.

We thoroughly reviewed everything: the lab results, the imaging, every detail. I personally ensured nothing was overlooked. You can take a deep breath now. You're in the clear and in great shape.

Now, I do want to point out one thing. Your cholesterol levels came back a bit high. It's nothing alarming, but it's something to keep an eye on. I'd recommend cutting back on greasy and fatty foods, maybe incorporating more heart-healthy options into your diet. It's a simple change, but it can make a big difference.

It's not every day I get to say, "You're cancer-free." Thank you for trusting me, and that we could give you clarity and peace of mind. You've got a lot of life ahead of you to look forward to. Now take care of yourself, and if you ever have any questions or concerns, I'm here to help.

The Longest Spelling Bee Ever

Synopsis: A person reflects on their childhood experience in an intense and unforgettable spelling bee, highlighting sibling rivalry, an unfair challenge, and the determination it took to make it through to the final rounds.
(Approx. 120 seconds)

It was the longest spelling bee ever. Or at least, that's how it felt. I still remember practicing with my brother every night leading up to it. He was two years older, already good at everything, and I just wanted to keep up. We drilled those words until my head spun, word after word, day and night. And then, finally, it was time.

Round after round, I kept getting my words right. So did my brother. It was nerve-wracking but exciting. And then came the word that turned the whole competition upside down: hamster. I spelled it perfectly. H-A-M-S-T-E-R. But the host shook her head and said, "That's incorrect. The correct spelling is H-A-M-P-S-T-E-R." My heart sank. Hampster? That couldn't be right. I knew it wasn't.

While the spelling bee went on, I ran to my classroom, ripped open my bookbag, and dug out the spelling bee book. There it was, clear as day: hamster. No P. I sprinted back to the auditorium, waving the book like it was evidence in a courtroom. The host apologized, said there had been an error, and put me back in the competition.

There was lots of cheering and excitement in the air at first, but the rounds kept going on and on. Kids were dropping out left and right until it was just me and my brother. The crowd eventually stopped cheering. Some even started booing. We were spelling word after word while everyone else just wanted to go home. Then the bell rang, and they ended it. "We'll finish this on Monday," the host said.

That weekend, my brother and I didn't practice together. We both wanted to win. On Monday, the tension was thick as we walked into the classroom for the final round. He spelled his first word, scissors, perfectly. I smiled and nodded. Then it was my turn: trousers.

T-R-O-W-S-E-R-S. "That's incorrect," the host said.

I was crushed but also... relieved. I was in the third grade, and truth be told, I was tired of spelling. And if I couldn't win, at least my big brother did. Watching him smile and hold that trophy? That felt like a win, too.

On the Scene

Synopsis: A paramedic arrives at the scene of an emergency, calmly assessing an elderly person's fall and managing the moment with empathy and professionalism. (Approx. 90 seconds)

Okay, ma'am, I'm here. My name is Alex, and I'm going to take care of you. You're awake, and that's a good sign. Just keep your eyes on me, nice and steady. You don't need to say anything: just stay with me.

Let me take a quick look at you. Okay, I see a bump on your head. I'm going to check your pupils real fast. Look at me... perfect. Alright, your pupils are reactive. That's a good sign. I'm going to check how you're doing. Just stay with me and keep those eyes open.

Alright, we've got a possible concussion. Let me check your pulse real quick... okay, that's a little high, but that's normal after a fall like this. I'm going to feel along your arms and legs now, just to make sure there's nothing broken. If anything feels wrong, I'll catch it. Just focus on staying calm.

You're doing great. Just keep breathing for me, nice and steady. I know this is scary, but you're not alone. We've got you.

Alright, we're going to get you onto the stretcher now. It might feel a little uncomfortable, but I promise we'll be gentle. Okay... one, two, three. There we go.

Okay, ma'am, we're in the ambulance now. I'm going to start an IV, just in case we need it later. You're doing so well. Just keep those eyes on me, alright? Don't drift off. Keep breathing steady and stay focused. Think about something you love, something comforting.

We're almost there. You're doing amazing. Just hang in there a little longer. You're in good hands, and we're going to get you through this.

The Heat of the Case

Synopsis: A detective interrogates a suspect in an arson case, pushing them to confess and reveal any accomplices. Despite overwhelming evidence, the suspect remains silent, and the detective reflects on their frustration and determination to get to the truth. (Approx. 90 seconds)

You're not going to say a word, huh? Fine. I've got all day. But let me lay it out for you. The evidence? It's screaming your name, even if you're sitting there stone-faced.

A witness pegged you that night, clear as day. Said they saw you lurking outside the shop. And the cameras? They don't lie. I've seen the footage myself. You were there, front and center.

You worked at that shop two years ago. Two years. What happened? Got let go? Or was it something more personal? Someone rub you the wrong way? Someone who needed a lesson?

You see, fires like this don't just pop up like that. Someone lights the match. And a fire that big? Someone else fans the flames. So, who's your partner?

Let me guess. You're sitting there, thinking if you keep quiet, it'll all go away. That we'll run out of steam. But here's the thing: we don't quit. This case? It's locked tighter than a safe. And when the jury sees it, they're not going to care that you sat here playing mute. They'll see the facts. They'll see you.

But you talk now, and perhaps you save yourself a little. Give me a name. A lead. Something. Because whoever you're covering for? They're not covering for you. When the heat turns up, everyone looks out for themselves. You know that better than anyone.

So, what's it going to be? Keep playing tough? Alright. I've been in this room before, and I'll be here when you're ready to break. Because you will. They all do. And when that moment comes, I'll be waiting for you.

Not In My Classroom

Synopsis: A teacher silences a classroom of teasing students and delivers a heartfelt, life-changing lesson on compassion and kindness. Addressing the importance of treating others with respect, she reflects on morals and challenges her students to become better individuals. (Approx. 90 seconds)

Enough! Quiet down. Right now.

Let me make one thing clear: this behavior will not be tolerated in my classroom. Making fun of someone because of their shoes or appearance is not just unkind: it's unacceptable. We don't laugh at others here, and we don't tear people down.

Do you know what it takes to walk into a room knowing you might be teased for something you can't control? That takes strength. And it takes even more strength to be the person who chooses compassion instead of being cruel.

You don't know what someone's going through at home. You don't know their story. So how dare you make it harder for them? I doubt your parents would be proud if they heard about this behavior.

The measure of who you are isn't in your clothes or what you own, it's in how you treat others. One day, you'll look back on this and remember how your words and actions made someone feel. Will you be proud of that?

From this moment on, we do better. This classroom is a safe place. A place where everyone is treated with respect. If you can't do that, you're in the wrong room. Now, take a moment. Think about the kind of person you want to be. I know you have what it takes, but I better not see this behavior in my classroom ever again. Do I make myself clear?

Ripple Effect

Synopsis: A scientist confesses to their mother about going back in time to prevent their great-grandmother's tragic death. Hoping to change the course of their family's history, they share the unexpected consequences of their actions. (Approx. 90 seconds)

Mom, I need you to hear me out before you say anything. I thought I was doing something good. I thought I could make things better.

You've told me stories about Grandma, how she was never the same after her mom died in that bus crash. How it broke her. How that pain rippled down to you and shaped your whole childhood. I couldn't stop thinking about it. So, this time, I used the Time Machine to go back to 1957.

I found her too. Great-Grandma. She was right there at the bus stop, standing in the sunlight, looking like she had her whole life ahead of her. I didn't tell her what was coming; I couldn't. Instead, I struck up a conversation. I asked her for directions, pretended I was lost, and kept her talking just long enough for the bus to pull away. And it worked. She missed the bus.

But then everything spiraled. The bus she planned to get on didn't crash... but she decided to catch another bus. And that bus, Mom, it was far worse this time.

When I came back, I knew something was off. You weren't the same. Grandma wasn't the same. The light I thought I'd bring you? It was gone. The world felt heavier, colder. I made it worse.

And now, you're looking at me like I'm crazy. Like none of this could be real. But it is real. I thought I could fix it. I thought I could erase the pain and give you the life you deserved. But I see now... I must go back. I can't leave it like this. I have to try again, Mom. This time, I'll get it right. I have to.

Party of Two

Synopsis: After throwing a lavish birthday party that no one attended except for their best friend, a person reflects on their friendships, family, and self-worth. They pour their heart out to the only person who showed up, questioning everything, but ultimately find a glimmer of positivity. (Approx. 90 seconds)

No one likes me. That's the only conclusion I can come up with. I mean, look at this. Thousands of dollars on caterers, decorations, a DJ... I even rented this stupid building, and for what? For no one to show up to my birthday party.

I don't get it. I planned everything. I sent invitations out weeks in advance. I followed up. I made sure there'd be enough food, enough cake, enough... everything. And still, no one came.

My own family didn't even show up. Not one of them. Just a text saying, "Sorry, something came up." Something came up. For all of them? At the same time?

And my friends... were they ever really my friends? "I'm not feeling well." "Rain check?" "Oh, I forgot it was tonight." Do you know how humiliating it is to stand at the door, looking at the clock, thinking, "Maybe they're just late..." only for no one to walk in? Every excuse feels like another slap in the face.

I'm so upset right now, but I am glad you're here. At least I know I can count on you. I was starting to doubt myself, wondering if I did something wrong, if I wasn't a good enough friend.

But you showing up? It tells me that maybe it isn't me after all. Maybe I was just investing in the wrong people.

Well, friend, the food isn't going to eat itself. Hand me a chicken wing and a slice of cake. If there's one thing I'm not letting go to waste, it's the catering. DJ, hit the music! If it's just going to be us, we might as well make it a party to remember.

Moment of Truth

Synopsis: A parent reassures their child and delivers the news of their college acceptance. As they look online together, the parent reassures their child of their worth, regardless of the outcome, and ultimately shares the joyous news of their acceptance. (Approx. 90 seconds)

Okay, sweetheart, breathe. Just take a deep breath. I know you're nervous. Who wouldn't be?

But listen to me, no matter what this screen says, you are good enough. You hear me? You've worked so hard for this. Late nights, early mornings, putting in everything you had. That doesn't disappear if the answer isn't what we want. But let's not assume the worst, okay?

Alright, let's do this together. I'll check, and we'll see this through. But let me just say this first: I'm proud of you. So proud. Not because of any acceptance email but because of the person you've become. The kindness you show to others, the way you never give up even when things get tough... that's what matters most. And that's something no college decision can take away.

Alright, I'm logging in now. Here we go. Okay... are you sure you don't want to look? Alright, I'll tell you.

Sweetheart, you did it! You got in! Come here. Oh, I wish you could see your face right now.

This moment? This is yours. You earned this.

I'm so excited! My baby girl is going to college!

Worth the Wait

Synopsis: A woman shares a heartfelt conversation with her husband while waiting for the results of a home pregnancy test. She reflects on the pain of trying to conceive and the constant questions from others, culminating in a moment of shared joy. (Approx. 90 seconds)

I don't know if I can look. What if it's negative again? I mean, how many times can we keep doing this, hoping, and only seeing one line? It feels like... like I'm failing you. Like I'm failing us.

And it's not just the test. It's everything. The looks, the questions. "When are you having a baby?" "What are you waiting for?" As if we aren't trying. As if every "no" doesn't already sting.

And then there are the assumptions every time I gain a little weight. "Are you pregnant?" "Is it finally happening?" It cuts deeper than they know. Do you know how hard it is to smile and laugh it off when, inside, I'm breaking?

I know people mean well. They don't realize what they're doing. But it's like every time they ask, they're reminding me of something I might never have. And I try to stay strong. I do. But sometimes I wonder... what if it's not meant to be? What if there's something wrong with me?

Honey, you've been so patient and kind, and I love you for it more than I can say. But I know this has been hard on you, too, and I hate that. I hate how this has made us question ourselves, doubt everything, and feel so much pain. I hate that this test has so much power over us.

Alright, I'm going to look. I just... need a moment to breathe. Can you hold my hand? Alright. Here we go.

The Price of Kindness

Synopsis: A person recounts their frustrating experience with a neighbor to a grocery store clerk, reflecting on the state of the world when an unexpected act of kindness restores their faith in humanity. (Approx. 120 seconds)

Ms. Georgia, I've got to tell you what happened to me. I just needed a cup of flour. That's it. I was in the middle of making stew, thought I'd make some biscuits to go with it, and realized I was out. So, I went next door, thinking, hey, neighbors help each other out, right? At least, that's how it used to be.

But when I knocked, they just looked at me like I was asking for something outrageous. And then they said, "No. You can drive to the store and buy your own." Just like that. No hesitation, no "I'm sorry, I don't have any to spare." Just... no. I mean, who says that? It's a cup of flour!

I walked away feeling so disappointed. It's not even about the flour. It's about what it means. People don't help each other anymore. Everyone's so guarded, so focused on themselves. And I get it: maybe they've been burned, or they had a bad day. But still, it made me wonder: what happened to kindness?

I apologize for going on and on like this. I just needed to get it off my chest. It's been bothering me since I left their house.

Uh. Excuse me, sir? What are you doing? Ms. Georgia, did they really just pay for my flour? I can't believe it!

Thank you so much sir!

Wow. I didn't see that coming. After everything I was just saying... maybe kindness isn't gone after all. Maybe it's just quieter than it used to be.

Well, thanks for listening, Ms. Georgia. I'll bring you some of that stew later: and don't worry, I'll add a few biscuits too.

Shape Up or Ship Out

Synopsis: After new recruits attempt a practical joke, a drill sergeant delivers a powerful speech about discipline, respect, and the importance of being prepared for the challenges ahead. (Approx. 120 seconds)

Line up! Straighten those backs, eyes forward. Wilson, is that a smirk? Wipe it off your face.

Matthews, you think this is funny? You all think it's a good idea to waste my time with some childish prank? Let me make one thing clear: this isn't a playground. This is preparation. Preparation to defend your country, to stand for something bigger than yourselves. If you can't take this seriously, you're in the wrong place.

You think fighting for America is a joke? Let me tell you what's not funny. Watching someone freeze up in the field because they weren't ready. Hearing a mother cry because her son didn't come home. That's what's on the line here. That's why I'm hard on you. That's why this matters.

Johnson, your uniform is a mess. Fix it. Wilson, your salute looks like you're swatting a fly. Work on it. And Matthews, dragging your feet won't get you anywhere but last place. You're better than this... all of you. But you need to start acting like it.

Listen up. I don't yell because I'm angry. I don't push you because I enjoy it. I do it because I see what you can be. You have potential, but potential means nothing if you don't put in the work. Right now, you're wasting it.

You want to know what makes a great soldier? It's not strength. It's not speed. It's heart. It's the willingness to push through pain, to keep going when everyone else gives up. It's respect. For your team, for your mission, and for yourself. That's what I want to see in you.

So, here's the deal: no more pranks. No more slacking. You're here to become the best version of yourselves, not just for you but for the people counting on you. Stand up straight. Fix your gear. Show me you're ready to be the kind of soldier this country can be proud of.

Now, drop and give me twenty. And while you're down there, think about this: Are you going to rise to the occasion or fall by the wayside? The choice is yours.

Don't Walk Away

Synopsis: A person pleads with their significant other to stay, struggling to understand the sudden breakup. As they beg for closure, they confront their pain, love, and desperation for answers. (Approx. 90 seconds)

I don't understand. I really don't. You said you could see a future with me. You told me I was the one. I met your family. Your mom hugged me like she already thought of me as part of the family. So, what changed? What happened between then and now?

You're telling me, "It's not you, it's me," but how is that supposed to help me? How is that supposed to make any of this make sense? I... I keep replaying everything in my head, trying to figure out where I went wrong. What did I do? Did I say something? Not say something?

Please, just tell me, and I'll fix it. I'll do whatever it takes. Just... don't walk away from us.

I'm sorry. I don't even know what I'm apologizing for, but I'm sorry. If I hurt you, if I made you feel like this was the only option... I'm sorry. I never wanted to be the reason you're unhappy.

But you're not even giving me a chance. You're just... leaving. And I... I don't know how to do this without you. You've been my everything. My rock. My person. And now, you're just going to up and leave with no explanation?

Please. I'm begging you. Talk to me. Give me something; anything. Because right now, all I have are questions. And it's tearing me apart.

You don't have to do this. We don't have to end like this. Do you even care? Please... don't go!

Pull Your Weight

Synopsis: A loving spouse speaks about their exhaustion and burnout, gently encouraging their partner to step up and work together as a team to restore balance and unity in their relationship. (Approx. 90 seconds)

We need to talk. I'm so tired, babe. I don't mean just physically, though I am that too: it's more than that. I'm carrying so much right now, and I feel like I'm doing it alone. I come home after a long day at work, and there's still more waiting for me. The dishes, the laundry, the cleaning... it's just too much. And I know you've been going through a lot. I see it. I feel it. And I've been trying so hard to give you space and be patient. But I'm running on empty.

I love you so much, sweetheart. I really do, but I need us to work together. I need you to help me carry this load because I can't do it all by myself anymore. It's not good for either of us, and I'm scared of what will happen if we keep going like this.

I'm not asking you to fix everything or do everything. I just need to feel like we're in this together. Like we're a team. Because when I look at you, I don't see someone who's lazy or doesn't care. I see someone who's grieving, who's overwhelmed. And I want to help you too, but I can't pour from an empty cup. I need you to meet me halfway. We need to find a solution because this can't continue.

I believe in us. I know we can figure this out together.

I Said Yes

Synopsis: A woman shares with her friend the unexpected joy of finding love and saying yes to a proposal after the loss of her husband. She reflects on her journey, the man who proposed, and the happiness she never thought she'd feel again at her age. (Approx. 75 seconds)

I said yes! Can you believe it? Me; the woman who promised she would never remarry. After Willy passed, I thought that was it for me. I had my great love story, and starting over felt... impossible. And yet, here I am, grinning like a schoolgirl with a ring on my finger.

Mark is wonderful. And, of course, you already know that. Everyone does: even my children, and you know how protective they are. They've been on board since the beginning. They kept teasing me, saying I blushed every time he walked into the room. Can you imagine? At my age?

He's kind and thoughtful, and the way he is with the grandkids? It's like he was created to be part of this family. He loves that I hum while I cook, that I can't start my day without peppermint tea, and even that I'm terrible at remembering where I put my glasses. He doesn't just accept me; he celebrates me.

I never thought I'd find love like this again. Mark reminds me every day just how special this second chance is. You know, it's funny. I used to think my story had ended. But now, I see there's so much more to come. And I'm so glad I get to share it with someone like him. I thought remarriage wasn't in the cards for me. I truly believed that chapter of my life was closed. But now I see, it's never too late to start over again.

Big Break

Synopsis: An actor reflects on the emotional toll of pursuing their passion, grappling with self-doubt, and the challenges of an industry where talent doesn't always guarantee success. (Approx. 90 seconds)

I'm trying, you know? Audition after audition, self-tape after self-tape. I'm giving it everything I have. Even my agent says my work is impeccable. But nothing. Not a callback, not a booking, not even a whisper of interest. And it's starting to make me wonder... is it me?

Am I not pretty enough? Am I too pretty? Should my hair be curly? Straight? Am I too tall? Too short? Too... much? It feels like I'm in some endless lottery where the odds are never in my favor. And the kicker? I'm watching people who barely try: who don't even care, get the jobs.

Meanwhile, I'm over here pouring my soul into this, and it feels like no one sees it.

I've blocked out events, just in case I book something. I've spent money I barely have on workshops, acting classes, headshots... all for what? To feel like I'm running on a treadmill that's going nowhere?

People keep saying, "Don't give up. It will happen. Don't focus on the booking; focus on the joy of the audition." Well, the joy doesn't pay the bills. The joy doesn't make the sacrifices feel any less heavy. And yet... there's a part of me that can't let it go. That still believes this is my purpose.

But right now? I don't know what to do. I don't want to quit, but I'm so tired of trying to convince myself that it'll all work out. How do you keep chasing something when it feels like it's running away from you?

Saved by a Cat

Synopsis: A person recounts how a stray cat ended up saving their life in a dramatic and unexpected way. Initially reluctant to take in the feline, they now realize the cat's impact goes far beyond companionship. (Approx. 75 seconds)

If you had told me a week ago that a cat would save my life, I wouldn't have believed you. Me? A cat person? Not in a million years. I was all about dogs. Loyal, energetic, always wagging their tails. Cats? They always seemed so unfriendly and detached. At least, that's what I believed; until she showed up.

This past Tuesday I was running late, rushing to get out the door. I grabbed my keys and was halfway to my car when she darted right in front of me, yowling like her tail was on fire. I almost tripped over the cat. I was so annoyed! I tried to shoo her away, but she wouldn't budge.

She just kept meowing, circling my legs. And then it happened, the crash.

A tree. A massive tree in my yard came down right where my car was parked. If I had been a second faster, I would have been inside it. I was frozen in my tracks. She just sat there, staring at me like, "You're welcome."

After that, I couldn't just leave her. I brought her inside, cleaned her up, gave her some food. Took her to the vet and got her shots. And now? She's got a name. Mittens; and a home. And somehow, her quiet little presence feels like a comfort I didn't know I needed.

The Weight of the Cape

Synopsis: A disheartened superhero wrestles with the decision to quit after feeling the world no longer deserves saving. Confronted by the chaos of Cardinal City and a manipulative villain, they must decide if hope is worth holding onto. (Approx. 75 seconds)

I've had enough. The cape, the powers, the endless pursuit of protecting this city; a place that seems to only thrive on chaos. It's time to let it go. Lightning speed, X-ray vision, bulletproof skin... and for what? Every time I stop one disaster, two more erupt. This place was supposed to be a beacon of light, but now? It's nothing but shadows. Our citizens are drowning in greed and hate. Cardinal City doesn't feel worth saving anymore.

There was a time when flying over the skyline meant something. When stopping a derailing train or catching a criminal felt like a victory. But now? I look through walls, through lies, through people, and all I see are cracks. Every hero has limits, and I think I've reached mine.

And then there's Phantom. Always one step ahead, turning the city against itself. He doesn't just destroy; he manipulates. He fuels the anger, the division, and the hopelessness. It feels like I'm fighting a losing battle. And if no one else cares, why should I?

But, if I walk away, who's left? When tragedy comes crashing down, and there's no one to hold the line, who will step forward? The villains are waiting to pounce, and if I quit now, the darkness wins. It's the kind of thought that won't let me rest. This city may be broken, but what if it still needs someone to fight for it?

I don't know... I just don't know if I'm the hero the city needs anymore.

Clean Comedic Monologues

Mother-in-Law's Big Moment

Synopsis: A bride recalls how her over-the-top mother-in-law almost stole the show at her wedding by wearing white, coughing during the ceremony, and catching the bouquet. (Approx. 1 minute 30 seconds)

I think my mother-in-law tried to ruin my wedding. At first, I thought I was just imagining it, but as the day went on, it became very clear, this woman had no interest in being the mother of the groom. She wanted to be the star of the show.

It all started when she walked in wearing white. I mean, really? You're gonna show up in all white to my wedding looking like a counterfeit bride?" But there she was, trying to steal the spotlight. They say imitation is the best form of flattery, so I didn't let it bother me too much, but that was just the beginning of the drama.

The pastor asked, "Is there anyone who objects to this union?" and before the Pastor could even finish the question, my mother-in-law started having a major coughing fit. She was so loud; she sounded like the little engine that could not. The cough echoed through the entire church, and for a moment, my future husband and I just looked at each other, like, is this really happening right now? I could feel myself getting ready to say something, but I knew if I opened my mouth, I'd end up on the nightly news, so I just smiled, took a deep breath, and decided I'd save the confrontation for another time.

But wait, it gets better. Fast forward to the bouquet toss. You know how the girls all gather around, hoping to catch it? Well, my mother-in-law didn't just join in. She sprinted to the front like the bouquet was an Olympic gold medal. She shoved my maid of honor out of the way with the force of a linebacker and somehow, someway, ended up with the bouquet.

I couldn't even be mad at that point. I was too busy laughing along with the other guests. She yelled out "I guess this means I'm next, huh?" and I'm sitting there, thinking, "No, ma'am, it absolutely does not mean that."

Eventually, we talked about her antics at the wedding, and to my surprise, she actually apologized. We're in a much better place now. I realized that if my husband has even half the commitment his mom showed chasing that bouquet, our marriage is going to last forever.

Eyes on the Prize

Synopsis: In a parking lot pep talk, a spouse hilariously rallies their partner to resist timeshare sales tactics and stay laser-focused on securing their free trip to Hawaii. (Approx. 90 seconds)

Alright, listen up. This is it; game time. We're about to walk into the lion's den, and I need you to have your game face on. No smiling, no nodding, no eye contact. If anyone asks, we are here strictly for the free trip to Hawaii, and that's it. I don't care if they offer us jet skis, lifetime coconut drinks, or the deed to a beachfront palace; we... are... not... buying... anything.

They're going to be charming. Oh, they'll be so nice. They'll show us pictures of their kids, Timmy in his soccer uniform, Little Susie baking cookies. Don't fall for it! Those kids probably don't even exist. They're trying to make us think, "Wow, timeshares are the best thing since sliced bread!" But let me remind you... we are a gluten-free family here. Heavy on the free!

Then, you'll see the hype people. Oh yes, professional clappers. They'll act thrilled about the deal, big smiles, nodding like bobbleheads. Don't look at them. They'll drag you in, and next thing you know, you'll be holding a brochure and considering "investment opportunities."

And the video montage? It'll be beautiful. Sunsets, frolicking couples, soft music. Remember, we frolic for free. We don't pay to vacay, so stay strong.

Last but not least, do not let them know what you're thinking. Put on your best poker face. If they think they've got us, they'll push harder. Smile too much? They'll smell weakness. Just keep saying, "Thank you, but we're not interested."

Alright, Hawaii is waiting. Let's do this!

The Pageant Fiasco

Synopsis: A reluctant beauty pageant contestant hilariously recounts their awkward journey through a pageant they didn't want to enter. (Approx. 120 seconds)

I never wanted to be in a beauty pageant. Apparently, the title "Governor's Daughter" is enough to qualify you, even if you've never set foot in a pageant before.

We started out with an opening group dance. It was awful. I might appear poised, but I have the coordination of a toddler on roller skates. I was supposed to step-ball-change, but I think I step-ball-fell at least three times.

Next came the swimsuit competition. All the other contestants had on bikinis, like they'd just walked out of a swimsuit magazine. And then there was me, wearing a one-piece bathing suit and a sarong to cover up the double cheeseburger I ate during the break. I'm not even gonna lie, at this point, I felt fierce and confident, and I certainly wasn't hungry like everyone else.

Then came the dreadful evening gown portion. I had on a stunning sequin dress with a 10-foot-long train. It was breathtaking. But here's the thing: I've never walked in heels. Like ever. So, the moment I stepped on stage, I tripped over the train and landed flat on my face. I tried to play it off by doing the worm, but maybe that wasn't the most graceful decision. The audience thought it was hilarious, but the judges didn't seem too amused.

After that came the talent competition. Now, I can't sing, I can't dance, and juggling is out of the question. So, I decided to make balloon animals. It surprisingly started off okay. I made a dog... or maybe it was a giraffe... hard to say. Then I tried to make a swan, but it popped. I startled some kids in the audience, so I improvised and made a balloon snake instead. It was literally just a long green balloon... but I held it up like it was a masterpiece. The crowd erupted in applause. I think it was because they felt sorry for me, but I'll take it.

Finally, it was the question round. They asked, "Why do you want to win this competition?" I didn't even try to fake it. I said, "Honestly? I don't. I care nothing about beauty or fashion. I care about people and the community." Then, the strangest thing happened next; I got a standing ovation. People were cheering like I had just cured world hunger.

I don't know how, but I ended up winning first runner-up. Although I didn't want to participate at first, I'm glad I competed. Plus, if anything happens to the winner, I'll be ready to step up... balloon animals and all.

When Hunger Strikes

Synopsis: A hungry employee shares a laugh-out-loud confession about their hangry meltdown at work and the chaos it caused. (Approx. 120 seconds)

I'm here to formally apologize for my behavior today. Normally, I'm the kind of person who holds the elevator for everyone, even the guy who's still in the parking lot. But today? Let's just say I was more fire-breathing dragon than your friendly neighborhood coworker.

It started with Billy. Sweet, innocent Billy, who was just chewing gum. But to my ears, it sounded like he was auditioning for a percussion band. I told him to spit out his gum or I would write him up for disturbing the peace. Then came all the office chatter. Everyone was talking so loudly. I don't know what was so funny, but at one point, I asked, "Are we working or running a D-list comedy club?"

At first, I thought I was just stressed. I had a few deadlines to meet but nothing unusual. Then it hit me: it was 3 p.m., and I hadn't eaten anything all day. Nothing. Not even a sip of coffee. Suddenly, it all made sense. I was hangry! I've always thought "hangry" was just an exaggeration, but today, I learned it's a full-on personality disorder.

I'm not proud of what happened next. My manager, Sarah, walked by with a fully loaded BBQ brisket sandwich. I won't confirm or deny this, but I may have asked if I could smell it.

I had to find food quickly because I could feel the irritation boiling within. So, I had the bright idea to find a vending machine. I thought a quick bag of chips would hold me over, but of course, the chips got stuck. I tried shaking it. gently at first; but then things escalated quickly.

The next thing I knew, the entire vending machine tipped over. And that, my friend, is why I'm sitting here in HR, explaining to you why there's a vending machine lying on its side in the break room.

If I still have a job tomorrow, I promise to take my lunch break on time and even pack a snack; maybe two, just to be safe. And, of course, I'll apologize to my coworkers for my actions. But let's be real, that vending machine probably had it coming.

The Art of Overthinking

Synopsis: A person attempts to meditate for 10 minutes, but racing thoughts and constant distractions turn it into a hilarious struggle. From chores to barking dogs, they just can't focus: but there's always tomorrow. (Approx. 90 seconds)

Alright, 10 minutes of meditation. I can do this. Turn off the TV. Eyes closed, block out all distractions. Deep breath in... and out. Okay, focus on the breathing. Just the breathing. In... and out. In... and, Did I pay the electric bill? I think I did. Wait, oh yeah, I'm meditating. Deep breath... in and out. I'll check the bill later. I'm sure it's fine.

Okay, back to my breathing. In... and out. Focus. This is about clearing my mind. I'm clearing my mind. Did I leave the laundry in the washer? Oh no, it's going to smell like wet socks. That's so disgusting. Okay, no, stop it. Stop it! Focus. Breathing. In... and out.

...Do we have milk? What else do I need from the store? Eggs, bread, toothpaste... no, stop making a grocery list in your head! Clear mind. Clear mind.

Deep breath. In... and out. And in... and. Was that a dog? Is the neighbor's dog barking again? Oh great, now I'm thinking about how loud Pongo is. Ugh. Focus. Breathe.

Oh no. Did I leave the oven on? What did I even use the oven for today? Oh wait, I haven't used the oven. Okay, false alarm. But what if there's a fire anyway? Should I check? No, I'm meditating. Everything is fine.

Deep breath. In... and, What am I supposed to be feeling right now anyway? Peace? Clarity? All I feel is... itchy. Why am I itchy? Did a mosquito get in here? Don't scratch. Okay, I scratched anyway.

Ugh! Why is this so difficult? Okay. Another deep breath. In... and out. Focus. Just breathe. In... and: Oh, look! My 10 minutes are up! That was... not relaxing. At all.

Well... I guess I'll try again tomorrow. They say practice makes perfect. Maybe I can make it to at least 2 minutes before the dog starts barking next time.

The Way to His Heart

Synopsis: A mother hilariously coaches her daughter on winning a man over through cooking. despite doing all the work herself. Determined to get her daughter married, she dishes out life lessons along with the food, making sure the guy believes her daughter is a master chef. (Approx. 90 seconds)

Alright, sweetheart, pay attention because this is how you land a husband. They say the quickest way to a man's heart is through his stomach, and tonight, we are serving up true love with a side of biscuits and gravy. Now, hand me that whisk. no, not like that! Gentle! Graceful!

Now, when he asks, you tell him everything was made from scratch. And say it with confidence!

If you hesitate, he'll know. Men can smell fear and store-bought from a mile away. Now, pass me the salt; no, not that one, darling, that's sugar! Lord, help us.

Listen, I know you "don't like cooking." But baby, you like love, don't you? You like romance? You like wedding rings? Because let me tell you, a plate of my smothered lamb chops has gotten more proposals than a Valentine's Day sale at a jewelry store.

Now, stir that gravy and nod like you know what you're doing, and don't forget to smile. Look a little tired, like you've been slaving away in this kitchen all day. Not too tired; you still need to look presentable. And in case he asks why you don't have flour on you, pat a little on your cheek. You need evidence, child!

Alright, now when you serve him, don't use paper plates. Bring out the fine china. Let him see the effort. And whatever you do, do NOT tell him I did this. I know you are an honest woman, so if he asks for the recipe, just smile and say, 'Oh, it's a family secret.' Because it is: my secret.

There, done. He's gonna take one bite and fall in love. And when he does, you better say 'yes' because I am NOT doing this again for another man. This kitchen is closed after the wedding!

The Prom Patrol

Synopsis: A strict prom chaperone takes the responsibility of maintaining order to the highest level, addressing the students with a firm set of rules before the night begins. (Approx. 90 seconds)

Stop the music! Ladies and gentlemen, before this night gets underway, I have a few important announcements. As your official prom chaperone, it is my sworn duty to ensure that tonight remains a classy, safe, and, most importantly; respectable event. That means there will be rules. Lots of them. And I expect full compliance.

First order of business: the punch. I have personally taste-tested it multiple times, and I will continue to do so throughout the night. If anything seems suspiciously fizzy, sour, or has a mysterious aftertaste, I will investigate further. You've been warned.

Now, let's discuss dancing regulations. Every couple must maintain a one-foot minimum distance at all times. That's twelve inches! That's the length of a sub sandwich! If I see anyone getting closer than a deli special, I will step in.

Effective immediately, the following songs are banned: anything with the words grind, bump, or slow. If a song makes me personally want to shimmy, it's out. If I hear one suggestive lyric, we're switching to a lovely instrumental playlist of thunderstorms and bird sounds.

And lastly, absolutely no sneaking out. This is a high school prom, not a prison break. If I see anyone heading toward the exits, I will assume you are attempting a heist and act accordingly. I have eyes everywhere.

Now that we've established order... let's have some fun!

The Black Friday Game Plan

Synopsis: A family prepares for the ultimate Black Friday shopping mission, mapping out strict rules and tactics to ensure they grab the best deals before anyone else. (Approx. 180 seconds)

Alright, family, listen up! Thanksgiving is over, which means it's go-time. Black Friday is not just a sale: it's a sport. And in this house, we play to win.

Rule number one: NO HEELS. I don't care how cute they are. This is not a fashion show; it's a battlefield. Sneakers only. Preferably something with a grip. If you slip in Aisle 5 reaching for a TV, you're on your own.

Rule number two: Do not wander off. We move as a unit. If you get lost, find the nearest employee and tell them the code word: "Clearance." They'll know what to do.

Rule number three: Cart strategy. One person drives, and one person grabs. No sudden stops, no getting blocked in. And if necessary, use the cart to gently assert dominance.

Rule number four: The buddy system. Nobody faces the electronics section alone. If you see a TV under $200, you yell, "GO TIME!" and we attack. And by attack, I mean circling the merchandise like a pack of hungry wolves and claiming it as ours.

Rule number five: Use distraction tactics. If someone else reaches for the last laptop, don't panic. Compliment their shoes, talk about the weather, ask them for the time, and when they look away for even a second, it's ours.

Rule number six: Check the fine print. Some of these deals are "limited quantity." Translation: "blink and you miss it." If the doors open at 5:00 AM, we are posted at the entrance by midnight, ready to sprint the second those doors open.

Rule number seven: No hesitation. If you think, you lose. If it's in your hands, it's yours. Debating between two items? Take both and decide later. This is not the time for second-guessing.

Alright, everyone clear? We trained for this. We've studied the ads, mapped the aisles, and visualized success. Now, take a deep breath, stretch, and remember: It's not about what we need: it's about what's 70% off.

LET'S GO!

Love and Allergies

Synopsis: A person recounts their Valentine's Day disaster to their best friend, as every romantic gesture from their crush triggers another allergic reaction. Despite the mishaps, a heartfelt note proves that love is worth it. (Approx. 150 seconds)

Okay, so you know how I've been crushing on Adam forever? Well, he finally worked up the nerve to ask me to be his Valentine. Super cute, right? I was so excited. I mean, what could go wrong?

Turns out... everything.

It started off sweet, literally. He showed up with this giant, heart-shaped box of chocolates. You know, the fancy ones wrapped in gold foil? Yeah, except I'm allergic to chocolate. So, I had to awkwardly thank him while discreetly shoving the box aside like it was a ticking time bomb.

But he had a backup plan, flowers! Gorgeous, vibrant, pollen-filled flowers. One deep breath and I'm instantly sneezing. My eyes watered, my nose ran, and suddenly I looked like I had been dumped instead of swept off my feet.

Adam must've sensed things weren't going great because next, he gave me the cutest stuffed bear. So soft. So cuddly. So,... made of wool. You see where this is going? I was now sniffling, sneezing, and breaking out in hives. Truly a Valentine's Day look for the ages.

Then came dinner. Fancy seafood restaurant, candlelit table, the whole nine yards. So romantic. But guess what? I'm allergic to seafood. And to make things worse, they had just run out of chicken. So, there I was, sitting at a five-star restaurant, contemplating if I should just order a plate of napkins.

At this point, he looked so defeated, but he had one more idea; ice cream. Cute, right? WRONG. Because, of course, I'm lactose intolerant.

He was so disappointed like he had completely ruined the day. But then, he handed me a little note that said:

"You might be allergic to everything, but I'd still choose you over anything."

And just like that, I melted. Not from the chocolate I couldn't eat or the flowers I couldn't smell, but from the way he cared enough to keep trying. Maybe Valentine's Day didn't go as planned, but I wouldn't change a thing because one thing is for sure: I might be allergic to a lot of things, but love isn't one of them.

Night Owl

Synopsis: A self-proclaimed night owl struggles to understand how anyone functions in the morning. Despite hearing all the advice about early birds and productivity, they simply can't wrap their half-asleep mind around the concept of waking up before noon. (Approx. 90 seconds)

Morning people confuse me. How do you wake up at sunrise and just... exist? Fully functional? Making breakfast? Speaking in full sentences?

They say the early bird gets the worm. Good for the bird. The bird can have all the worms. I don't even like worms, so how is that even a selling point?

Every morning, I set my alarm with the best of intentions. I tell myself, "Tomorrow, I'm going to be productive! I'll get up early, make coffee, go for a jog!" And then morning arrives, and my body files an immediate restraining order against consciousness.

I hit snooze so many times my alarm clock starts getting an attitude. It's like, "You sure about this? Do you really think five more minutes is gonna help?"

And then there are the morning people, the ones who just pop out of bed like toast and start doing things. They wake up happy. They go for a run. They make green smoothies. They send emails... on purpose. Meanwhile, I'm just over here trying to figure out which dimension I'm in.

And don't even get me started on those "rise and grind" people. I can't even "rise," let alone "grind." My "rise and grind" is more like "drag and survive."

Truly, I don't know what's worse, morning people or the fact that society expects me to be one.

Can we normalize the phrase "the well-rested night owl gets the snack?" Because that's a lifestyle I can fully support.

Until then... I'll see you this afternoon. Maybe.

Baby on Board

Synopsis: A taxi driver recalls a chaotic ride when a passenger thought she was in labor. With no medical training, panic set in, only for it to be a false alarm. (Approx. 120 seconds)

So, the other day, I thought I was about to deliver a baby. In my taxi. In the middle of traffic. With absolutely no qualifications aside from watching the occasional medical drama.

It started like a normal ride. The lady got in and told me she needed to go to the hospital, and I was like, "Sure, no problem." Then she said the four words no taxi driver ever wants to hear: "My water just broke."

I start panicking. I tell her to breathe, but I'm the one hyperventilating. In hindsight, I probably should've dialed 9-1-1, but instead, my brilliant first instinct was to pull over and start Googling 'how to deliver a baby in traffic.'

Of course, Google was no help. Step one: 'Remain calm.' Too late for that! Step two: 'Prepare a clean, sterile environment.' Sure, let me just grab the disinfectant wipes I don't have. Step three: 'Use warm towels to keep the baby comfortable.' Really? The only towels I have are fast-food napkins and one sweaty gym towel under the seat!

At this point, I just try my best to keep her calm. "Ma'am, we're gonna get through this. Just hang in there! Hold the baby in!"

And then... just like that, she stops. Looks at me. Totally calm. Then goes, "Oh. Wait. I think... I think it was just my water bottle."

Ma'am. What?

"Yeah, it must've tipped over when we hit that bump. Wow, that could've been embarrassing!" Could've been? I was seconds away from quitting my job, changing my name, and living off the grid. I just sat there, holding the wheel like it was my emotional support system, while she patted my shoulder and asked if I was okay.

I was speechless.

Long story short, I took her to the hospital... and from now on, I have officially banned all water bottles from my taxi.

Tall Tales

Synopsis: The speaker tells a hilarious story about a man whose height mysteriously increased over time. After confronting him, they realize honesty matters way more than a few extra inches. (Approx. 90 seconds)

I met this guy a while back: super nice, funny, great conversation. He told me he was 5'8". Cool, sounds good to me. Then, a few months later, I overheard him telling someone he was 5'11".

Okay... maybe I misheard him the first time.

Then, last week, he introduced himself to someone as six-foot-one. At this point, I'm looking at him like, "Sir, are you on a growth spurt I need to know about?"

And then, yesterday, this man looked me dead in the eye and said, "Yeah, I'm about 6'3" now." At this rate, he'll be 6'7" by next week and getting drafted by the Lakers.

I had to step back and ask myself, do men think there's a minimum height requirement for dating? Like a roller coaster sign that says, "Must be this tall for a relationship"? Because the way some of them act, you'd think being under six feet was the ultimate deal breaker.

So, I finally called him out. I looked right up at him; okay, directly in front of him, and said, "You don't have to lie about your height. You are perfect just the way you are."

He laughed, admitted he got carried away... then he unexpectedly asked me out.

I said yes! His height is no issue as long as he keeps it 100 with me. When it really comes down to it, true love should be measured in character, not centimeters.

The Professional Complainer

Synopsis: A family member complains about everything, from gas prices to the weather, while somehow affording luxury vacations. (Approx. 90 seconds)

I have a family member who complains for sport. Like, if there were an Olympic event for finding something wrong with anything, they'd have a gold medal and a sponsorship deal.

Gas prices? Too high. Grocery prices? Outrageous. Eggs? "Might as well start my own farm at this point!" The weather? If it's cold, it's too cold. If it's hot, it's "unbearable." I once heard them sigh at a perfectly pleasant 72 degrees.

And money. Oh, they love to talk about money. How they "don't have any," how "the struggle is real," how they're "just trying to survive." But next thing you know, they're posting selfies from a 5-star beach resort in Spain.

I asked, "Wait, didn't you just say you were broke?" And they hit me with, "Yeah, but I needed this trip for my mental health!" Oh, okay, so vacations are free now? Because last time I checked, flights, hotels, and beachside smoothies weren't covered by 'the struggle.'

But the real moment that got me? The other day, they were complaining about how expensive it is to exist, while holding a $7 coffee. Just ranting about the "cost of living" between sips of an oat milk caramel drizzle macchiato with extra foam.

Enough was enough!

So, I did something bold. I said, "Hey, what if we, I don't know... appreciated what we have for a second?"

They actually paused. No complaints. Just silence. For like... five whole seconds.

Hey, I'll take what I can get. Progress is progress.

The Potluck Predicament

Synopsis: Skeptical of potlucks, an employee finally participates. only to get trapped in office politics when the boss insists they try their horrifying meatloaf. (Approx. 90 seconds)

I have never been a fan of potlucks. Too many variables. I barely trust buffets, and now I'm supposed to trust Gary from HR to properly wash his hands before making his "famous" sweet potato pie. Hard pass.

But this time, I caved in. I made some deviled eggs, and let me tell you, they were a hit. People were practically fighting over them. I was feeling good. Until I saw what the boss brought.

It was a meatloaf. Or at least, that's what they called it. But it looked inedible. Like something that should come with a biohazard label. It had an unnatural grayish tint and somehow managed to both crumble and ooze at the same time.

Then it happened. The boss locked eyes with me. "Have you tried my dish yet?"

Now, under normal circumstances, this is where I fake a phone call, pretend I have food allergies, or suddenly remember I'm fasting. But I'm up for a promotion, and I don't know if refusing to eat my boss's mystery meat would be considered "poor team spirit."

So, I did what had to be done. I took a bite. And immediately regretted every decision that led me to this moment.

It tasted like she tried to season sadness, like it had been microwaved in defeat, and basted in broken dreams.

I forced a smile. "Mmm! So... unique!"

She smiled from ear to ear. "It's my grandmother's secret meatloaf recipe!" Well, based on the taste, it should've been kept a secret.

To sum it up, I got the promotion, but next time, the only thing the boss is allowed to contribute is paper plates; and maybe soft drinks if we're feeling generous.

Diagnosis Everything

Synopsis: A friend has taken diagnosing to a whole new level, diagnosing everything from minor sneezes to malfunctioning Wi-Fi. Their concerned friend tries to bring them back to reality. (Approx. 75 seconds)

Listen, I say this with love, but we might need to stage an intervention. Because you diagnose everything. And I mean everything.

I sneezed once, and you said, "Seasonal allergies." Sneezed twice? "Early-onset pneumonia."

The other day, I had a headache. A normal person would say, "Drink some water." But no, not you. You hit me with, "Might be a brain tumor." Turns out I just needed a nap. But sure, let's jump straight to the worst-case scenario!

And it's not just people. Your car made a weird noise, and instead of taking it to a mechanic, you diagnosed it with "transmission failure and a hint of carburetor distress." It was a loose screw!

Your phone froze yesterday, and you whispered, "Early signs of software deterioration." No, you just need to delete some of your old selfies.

Look, I know you mean well, but we have got to reel this in. You're out here diagnosing doorknobs and Wi-Fi signals.

One day, you're going to be right about something; but until then, I need you to go outside and get some sunlight. Maybe step away from WebMD for a while.

Dad Rules

Synopsis: A father has an intimidating talk with his daughter's first date while she gets ready. As he lays down the law, strict curfews, no handholding, and absolutely no kissing: he somehow manages to keep the poor boy both terrified and thoroughly confused. (Approx. 90 seconds)

Alright, young man, take a seat. Let's go over some ground rules while my princess finishes getting ready. First things first. she's back home by 9 p.m. sharp. Not 9:01, not 9:02. If my clock hits 9:03 and she isn't home, I will call the police, and you better hope they find you before I do.

Second, hands to yourself. I don't care if there's an earthquake and she's about to fall into a bottomless pit; you let gravity do its job. No holding hands, no arms around shoulders, and if you even think about leaning in for a kiss, think again.

Third, I've already run a background check. You seem clean; for now. But I'm watching. I got cameras, I got contacts, and I got a sixth sense when it comes to teenage foolishness. If anything goes sideways tonight, I'll know before you even drop her off.

Now, I understand you're just going to the movies, but let me be very clear. You are watching the movie. Not watching her. Not whispering in her ear. Not smiling in her face. You are sitting there, eyes forward, hands where I can imagine them, and enjoying the movie in silence.

If you follow these very simple and completely reasonable rules, we won't have any problems. Got it?

Drivers Ed

Synopsis: After repeatedly failing, a driver's ed student struggles with cones, parallel parking, and basic driving skills before finally passing on the fourth attempt: just barely. (Approx. 90 seconds)

You ever meet someone who failed driver's ed three times? Well, hi. Nice to meet you.

I thought driving would be easy: sit in the seat, press the pedals, and don't hit anything.

Simple. Until I realized that just because I watched people drive, it didn't mean I knew how to do it.

My first test started off strong, I adjusted the radio before adjusting the mirrors. Priorities, right? Then came the cones. You know, the ones set up for practice? I hit every single one. It looked like a demolition derby but with cones instead of cars.

Parallel parking? Forget it. I didn't park next to the curb: I parked on it. Fully. The instructor just wrote something down and whispered, "I need a new job."

Fast forward to my second attempt. I told myself; you've got this. I did not. I ran a stop sign, nearly took out a mailbox, and somehow ended up in a Taco Bell parking lot. I don't even remember making the turn.

Third attempt? I was so nervous I forgot to buckle my seatbelt. Automatic fail. Didn't even get to drive.

By my fourth try, I was practically a local legend. "Oh, you're that kid?" Yep. That's me. But this time, I was determined. I adjusted my mirrors, stopped at all the stop signs, and when it came time to parallel park... I nailed it. The instructor actually clapped. Probably out of shock.

Do I drive confidently now? Let's just say pedestrians should stay alert. But I passed, and that's what matters, right?

Grocery Store Code of Conduct

Synopsis: A parent lays out the ground rules before stepping foot in the grocery store, determined to keep the trip smooth and tantrum-free. (Approx. 90 seconds)

Alright, kiddo, listen up. We are about to enter the grocery store, and I need you to be on your best behavior. I am not going to be that parent running through the store after their kid; not today.

First off, we are here for groceries only. Not for toys, not for games, and definitely not for candy. If it's not on the list, it's not coming home. Asking me over and over won't change my mind, so don't even try it.

Now let's talk about hands. Do not touch anything unless I say so. This is a grocery store, not a petting zoo. If I don't tell you to pick it up, you don't need to go anywhere near it. Remember, I have eyes in the back of my head.

Now, listen carefully: You get one free sample per station. One. You will not act like you haven't been fed in days and circle back for seconds, thirds, or try to convince the sample lady you're a completely different child. We already ate before we left.

And you better act like you've got some home training. There will be no running, sliding, or cart joyriding. This is a grocery store, not a playground. If you so much as think about throwing a temper tantrum, just remember; I will drop my basket and start breakdancing right in aisle five. And trust me, I won't be the one who's embarrassed.

Here's the deal: if we make it through this trip without any incidents, there will be a treat at the end. So, remember, don't touch anything, don't ask for anything, and don't even look at anything. We are on a mission.

Now let's get these groceries and go!

Fame Looks Good on Me

Synopsis: A starry-eyed dreamer imagines life as a celebrity, money, luxury, and worldwide fame: until reality makes them rethink if it's really worth it. (Approx. 90 seconds)

I was made for fame. Some people are born to blend in. I was born to be on a billboard. My face? Perfect for magazine covers. My name? Screams A-list superstar. I can already hear it now: "Coming up next, a very exclusive interview with the one and only... Elizabeth Star!"

Oh, and the lifestyle? Top-tier. Pulling up in a luxury car that costs more than a house. Dripping in diamonds so heavy my wrist needs a personal assistant just to hold it up. Custom designer outfits flown in from Paris. And let's not forget the paparazzi! "No pictures, please!": but I will be secretly enjoying every moment.

And endorsements? Oh, I'll endorse everything. Fragrances, restaurants, fancy bottled water from the French Alps. Imagine my face on a shampoo bottle. ' For luscious, star-powered locks, use MY shampoo. Available nowhere near your budget!'

But hold on: what if I run to the store in sweatpants and no makeup, and suddenly I'm being bashed in the blogs? Or what if every distant cousin I've never met suddenly needs a loan? I mean, I love generosity, but I don't want to be a walking ATM. And personal space? Forget about it. Do celebrities even get to eat messy burgers, or is it all quinoa and caviar forever?

You know what? I'm realizing fame might be a little overrated. True happiness is not about money, cars, clothes, or expensive drinking water. It's about being content with who you are on the inside.

But let's be real. if someone offers me a million dollars to smile on a billboard, you better believe I'm striking a pose!

Stand-Down Comedy

Synopsis: A first-time stand-up comedian takes the stage with high hopes and terrible jokes. From botching the city name to bombing with classic joke setups, they power through an increasingly awkward set. (Approx. 90 seconds)

Houston, let's make some noise!!

Wait a minute... this is Dallas, isn't it? Awkward. Well, I'm off to a good start.

I need you all to clap it up for me. It's my first time doing stand-up, and I'm a little nervous. Alright, let's get into it. People always want to know why the chicken crossed the road. I'm like, who cares? As long as it gets to the other side... of my plate.

"Tough crowd. Must be a lot of vegetarians in here. Okay, okay, I got another one. So, I was driving the other day when I got pulled over by a cop. They asked me if I knew why I was being pulled over. I couldn't think of anything. They told me my taillight was out. I said, 'Officer, I didn't even know my car had a tail. Do I need to see a doctor about that?

... Now you know that was funny.

"Wow. Alrighty then, Let's see. Umm. Y'all ever notice how grandmas are supposed to know how to cook? Like, everyone wants to eat their grandmother's cooking, right? Not my grandma. It's so bad her dog won't even eat her food. She cooked the other day, and I tried to give it to Rover under the table. He sniffed it, looked me dead in the eye, and slid his bowl back like, 'Nah, I'm good fam.'

(Nervous Laugh)

I see we've got a heckler in the house! You want me to get off the stage? Look, I'd leave, but my ego is glued to this microphone. And besides, I paid $20 for parking."

Alright, alright, that's my time! Or at least, I think it is. I'm pretty sure I saw the host nodding off a few minutes ago. Raymond, wake up!

Thank you, Houston! I mean Dallas... Good night!

Teatime

Synopsis: A first-time golfer takes on 18 holes with nothing but confidence and a complete lack of skill. From misunderstanding tee time to causing mayhem on the course, their day is filled with accidents, exhaustion, and one very lucky bird. (Approx. 90 seconds)

So, I played golf for the first time. And let me tell you, this sport is not for the weak. Or the uncoordinated. Or anyone who values their dignity.

First off, I showed up for tee time, walked into the clubhouse, and asked for chamomile. The guy looked at me like I had just insulted his entire bloodline. Apparently, 'tee time' does not involve actual tea. Who knew?

I started the day thinking, 'I'll just walk the course! Get some exercise, take in the fresh air.' By hole three, I realized two things: One, golf courses are massive. And two, my legs are not built for this. So, I got a cart. And that's when things really went downhill; literally. Let's just say I may have underestimated the speed of a golf cart and overestimated my ability to turn. Ever seen a person take a corner so badly they end up in a sand trap? Well, now you have.

Then there was my 'birdie' moment. I lined up the shot, gave it everything I had, and the ball took off: right along with an actual bird. It was like slow motion. Feathers everywhere. I thought I had ended its career, but don't worry, it shook it off and flew away. Pretty sure it gave me a dirty look, though.

At one point, my ball went straight into the water. And because I didn't know any better, I went in after it. Good news: I found the ball. Bad news: I also found out that golf shoes are not made for swimming. One step in, and I went down like a sinking ship.

Anyway, 18 holes later, I lost six balls, bruised my ego, and made one bird question its life choices. Golf? Not as easy as it looks. Next time, I think I'll start with mini golf before trying to go pro.

Sedated

Synopsis: Fresh out of wisdom teeth surgery and still under anesthesia, a patient hilariously struggles to make sense of reality while talking to their mom. (Approx. 90 seconds)

Mom! Mom! Am I alive? Be honest. Blink twice if I didn't make it.

Wait... why are you laughing? This is serious. I can't feel my face. Did they take my whole face?

Do I still have a face?!

Why are you recording me? This is a medical emergency, not a family documentary. You're gonna put this on the internet, aren't you? Don't do this to me. I don't want to go viral. Fun fact, did you know viral rhymes with spiral, and spiral rhymes with...

Hold on: where are my teeth? I had teeth when I walked in. Now I don't. That's theft! Somebody call 9-1-1. I need my teeth back.

Wait, did I tell the nurse I loved her? Oh no. She gave me apple juice, and I think I proposed.

Was she cute? Do I have a new wife?

Mom, I'm starving. They said no solid food for days. DAYS! Do they think I can survive on Jell-O and suffering? Because I can't. I need a chicken sandwich.

Okay, I'm getting sleepy now. Can you wake me up when I stop embarrassing myself? Or at least when you delete that video.

Hands Off My Lunch

Synopsis: A determined office worker turns full-on detective after discovering their clearly labeled food has been stolen from the breakroom fridge. With over-the-top interrogations, wild accusations, and dramatic conclusions, they're determined to crack the case: no matter how ridiculous it gets. (Approx. 90 seconds)

Alright. Listen up. Someone in this office committed a crime today. A heinous crime.

I brought my lunch. I labeled my lunch. I double-checked that my lunch was securely in the fridge. And yet... when I went to retrieve it, do you know what I found? Nothing. The container? Gone. The evidence? Eaten. The betrayal? Unmatched.

So now, I have no choice but to launch a full investigation. And I will not rest until justice is served.

Let's start with the obvious suspect, Carlos. Oh, you conveniently brought lunch from home today? And yet, I see no evidence of Tupperware. No crumbs. Nothing. Very Suspicious.

Then we have Melissa. Always on a diet... until my food mysteriously vanishes. Interesting how your 'cheat day' lined up perfectly with the day my spaghetti disappeared. Coincidence? I think not.

And then... there's Michael. The silent snacker. Never admits to being hungry. Never brings food. And yet... he never starves. A true mystery. What's your secret, Mike?

Oh, so suddenly, everyone's got memory loss? Nobody saw a thing? Nobody heard a microwave beep? Fascinating. Sounds like we have a classic case of selective amnesia.

You know what? Fine. Enjoy your stolen meal. But just know... next time, I'm bringing extra hot sauce. You've been warned.

Runaway Fail

Synopsis: A sibling recalls the time their sister tried to run away after getting caught sneaking cookies. Mom and Dad played along, knowing she wouldn't make it past the driveway. (Approx. 120 seconds)

Do you remember the time you tried to run away? You were nine years old, and it lasted all of five minutes. It's easily one of my favorite childhood moments.

We were all sitting at the dinner table when it happened. Mom found out you ate all the cookies. She had specifically told us not to. I would've felt bad for you, but truthfully, I was just glad she didn't know I had one, too.

She hit you with the classic: "Since you don't listen, you're on punishment."

You were so mad at Mom. Was the punishment deserved? Absolutely. But in your mind, it was the greatest injustice of all time. So, you did what any rational, level-headed nine-year-old would do, you decided to run away.

You stomped upstairs, packed your tiny suitcase with the essentials: three shirts, one sock, your favorite toy, and: for some reason, a spoon. I don't know where you thought you were going, but apparently, a single spoon was a necessity.

The funniest part? Mom helped you pack. No tears, no begging you to stay. Just, "Here, don't forget your toothbrush." Dad barely looked up from the table. He just said, "Good luck out there, champ." I couldn't believe my ears.

At this point, I was getting worried. You looked at me like this was the last time we'd ever see each other. You marched down the driveway, fully committed to your new life. And then... you smelled dinner. Mom had made your favorite. Turns out, running away on an empty stomach? Not ideal.

So, you did the only logical thing. You turned around, walked back in, and sat down like nothing happened. Nobody said a word. Dad just passed you a plate.

That day, you learned two important lessons: never run away without eating first. And if you're going to take all the cookies, at least wait until after dinner.

The Cheapest Dad Ever

Synopsis: A hilarious look back at all the times Dad was being cheap, even when he didn't have to. From questionable budget-friendly choices to his lifelong commitment to "saving for a rainy day," they can't help but ask: Dad, why are you like this? (Approx. 90 seconds)

Dad, I gotta ask... why are you so cheap? No, really. I need answers. Because at this point, it's not about saving money; it's a lifestyle.

Remember when I lost my first tooth? Most kids got a crisp dollar from the tooth fairy. You slipped a dime under my pillow and said, "Don't spend it all in one place." What was I supposed to buy, Dad? A piece of gum from 1942?

Or how about the time we went to the movies, and instead of buying snacks like normal people, you popped popcorn at home, packed it into plastic baggies, and passed them out like we were running a bootleg concession stand? Not gonna lie; it was good, but I spent the whole movie nervous we'd get caught.

And let's talk about the thermostat, Dad. Why did you act like adjusting the temperature would bankrupt the family? It could be 10 degrees outside, and you'd be like, 'Just put on another layer.' I had so many layers on, I'm pretty sure if I fell over, I wouldn't have been able to get back up.

Oh, and vacations? We never flew. Ever. It was road trips or nothing. And if it wasn't a discount deal, we weren't going. I remember you avoiding toll roads at all costs. You called it highway robbery. Instead of paying a few bucks, we'd take the 'scenic route,' which was just Dad's way of saying we were about to add an unnecessary hour and a half to our trip.

But you were a good dad. A cheap dad, but a good one. And honestly, I respect it. I used to roll my eyes at your penny-pinching ways, but now, I'm proud to be just like you, clipping coupons, dodging extra charges, and refusing to pay full price for anything if I can help it.

Conclusion

As you close this first volume of Clean Cuts, I hope you've discovered monologues that resonate with your values, challenge your creativity, and inspire your passion for storytelling. Whether you're using these pieces to prepare for auditions, practice your craft, or perform on stage or screen, remember that your voice as an actor is powerful and unique.

This collection was crafted to empower performers to shine with authenticity and integrity. It offers material that reflects faith-inspired themes and clean, meaningful storytelling.

Acting is more than memorizing lines: it's about bringing characters to life, connecting with audiences, and sharing stories that uplift and inspire. And if you're not an actor but simply love engaging with powerful stories, I hope these monologues have offered you moments of reflection, laughter, and inspiration.

I encourage you to take what you've learned here and keep honing your craft with excellence and purpose. May God bless you as you pursue your passion, and may your journey as a performer be filled with opportunities to grow, connect, and shine.

Thank you for letting me be a small part of your journey. I look forward to sharing even more with you in future volumes. Keep shining and creating with heart, integrity, and boldness.

Appendix: Tips for Performing Monologues

Acting is a craft that blends skill, heart, and creativity. Whether you're preparing for an audition, rehearsing for practice, or sharing your talent with an audience, here are some tips to help you bring these monologues to life:

1. Dive Into the Character

Every monologue has a story to tell. Take a moment to imagine the character's backstory and the situation they're in. Ask yourself:
- Who are they speaking to?
- What do they want to express?
- What emotions are driving them in this moment?

The more you understand the character, the more authentic your performance will feel.

2. Make It Your Own

These monologues are a starting point for your creativity. Bring your unique perspective to the performance by drawing from your own experiences. Personalizing the material helps you connect deeply with the character's emotions and story.

3. Practice with Purpose

Rehearsal is where you build confidence and uncover the layers of the character. Whether you're practicing in front of a mirror, recording yourself, or sharing with a trusted friend, take time to focus on these key elements:
- Pacing: Let the words breathe so the emotions can settle with the audience.
- Vocal Variety: Play with tone and inflection to highlight the emotional shifts in the monologue.
- Body Language: Use your whole body to bring the character's feelings to life, not just your voice.

The more intentional your practice, the more natural and impactful your performance will feel.

4. Adjust for the Platform

Whether you're preparing for stage, TV, or film, it's important to adapt your performance to fit the platform:
- For Stage: Speak clearly and use larger movements to ensure your emotions reach every corner of the audience.
- For Film/TV: Focus on subtle expressions and natural gestures to draw viewers into the character's world.

5. Let the Material Shine

One of the things I love about these monologues is that they're free from profanity or suggestive content. This allows the focus to remain on the character's story and emotions. Lean into that purity and let the storytelling shine!

---

6. Seek God's Guidance

If you're performing a faith-based monologue, take a moment to pray and reflect before diving in. Trust that God has given you this talent for a reason, and let your performance be a way to glorify Him and inspire others.

Acting is about more than just delivering lines: it's about connecting with the heart of the story and sharing it in a way that resonates with others. I hope these tips encourage you as you grow in your craft and pursue your passion with excellence and integrity.

About the Author

Grace Covington is an actress, writer, singer, and digital creator from Richmond, Virginia. She is passionate about bringing stories to life with depth, authenticity, and purpose. Now based in Houston, TX, she has spent the past nine years crafting compelling, faith-driven narratives that resonate across generations. Her work in film, television, and digital media reflects a commitment to storytelling that uplifts, entertains, and inspires.

From stage to page, Grace brings creativity to every platform, proving that powerful stories don't need to compromise values to make an impact. Clean Cuts: Volume 1 is a testament to her dedication to high-quality, clean storytelling. demonstrating that both comedy and drama can be captivating, thought-provoking, and deeply meaningful.

Connect with Grace on Social Media:
@GraceFullyVlog on Facebook, TikTok, Instagram, and YouTube

For bookings and professional inquiries, contact:
GraceLeronePublishing@gmail.com

www.ingramcontent.com/pod-product-compliance
Lightning Source LLC
Chambersburg PA
CBHW070755120626
46557CB00002B/610